JEWS IN CHINA:

A HISTORY OF STRUGGLE

Nicholas Zane

To my sister, Isabelle

CONTENTS

ACKNOWLEDGMENT

To the list of people below — Simon Li; Ronald Leopold; Jan Erik Dubbelman; Elena Hesse & Andrew Rattue; Peter Oppenheimer; Catherine Oppenheimer; Gillian Perry — and the many others who have supported me in my hitherto short journey regarding Jewish people in China, I would like to express my utmost gratitude. This list below does not quantify this gratitude and put them in order, but is based chronologically on the date of our encounters.

I met Simon Li, executive director of the Hong Kong Holocaust and Tolerance Centre, at Yom HaShoah 2018, which he organized at the Ohel Leah Synagogue. At this event, I was intrigued by Jewish solidarity in Hong Kong and became even more fascinated by Jewish history. Since then, Simon and I have worked together extensively. I often do research and editorial work relating to politics for him, despite the distance barrier. Simon has also helped develop me academically and personally, as he guides me through my personal projects relating to the Jews in China, and any other historical topics which I found interesting. Simon is not only an academic mentor, but a dear friend whom I hope to work with more in the future.

I was invited by the South China Morning Post to interview Ronald Leopold, executive director of the Anne Frank House. Speaking to and writing about him at length inspired me quite a great deal — his passion for combating anti-

Semitism was apparent, and it made clear why he had dedicated his career to humanitarian causes as such. He invited me to the Anne Frank House in the summer and introduced me the Anne Frank House staff, allowing me to establish a formidable network.

Jan Erik Dubbelman, head of international development of the Anne Frank House, has been a part of the team since 1989. I met him at the Anne Frank House in 2018 and have since remained in touch. Jan Erik has provided me with many great opportunities, not least an invite to the Anniversary of the Anne Frank Declaration in the House of Parliament, Westminster. Jan Erik has a mission to help spread the word of Anne Frank to countries in which Holocaust education is niche, and I very much hope to help him do this by inspiring other people my age to start early; I hope to do Jan Erik's vision justice.

Andrew Rattue is my school's principal and Elena Hesse is my school's vice principal. Both of them have been extremely helpful and supportive of me and my projects outside of school, from helping facilitate the International Holocaust Memorial Day to allowing Leaver's Absence to attend important events. Their guidance has made sure that I maintained a state of academic excellence whilst never neglecting adventures beyond the International Baccalaureate program. To them, and all of the St. Clare's staff, I have only gratitude and thanks.

Peter Oppenheimer is the governor of my school — St. Clare's, Oxford. A German of Jewish descent, his family moved to England during the Second World War, although he lost many relatives to the atrocious Holocaust War Crimes. Despite his extensive career and expertise in a variety of fields, Peter is humble and energetic like few others. Peter has given me a great deal of support on my research about the Kaifeng Jews and connected me with experts in the field. Sometimes, our conversations in German also goes to develop my German skills. A fellow of Christ Church, Oxford since 1967 and former President of the Oxford Centre for Hebrew and Jewish Studies, Peter is someone I hope to continue receiving guidance from in pursuit of a future career in academia and politics.

Catherine Oppenheimer is the Chairman of the Oxford Council of Christians and Jews, an interfaith movement. Overwhelmingly warm and welcoming, Catherine has done much to widen my reach regarding the stories of Jews in China. My first lecture, given at the Oxford Jewish Community Centre, was hosted by Catherine — my adventures as a student 'lecturer,' if you will, formally began here, and hopefully will continue much further.

Gillian Perry was awarded the order of Chivalry Member of the British Empire by Prince Charles for a very good reason — as founder of the Anne Frank Trust UK, she has done much to promote Holocaust education and make the world a more pleasant place for Jews and other minority groups. I met Gillian at the Anniversary of the Anne Frank

Declaration in House of Parliament. Since then, despite having a full schedule, Gillian has done much to support and champion for me. Jewish rival newspapers, Jewish News & Jewish Chronicle, both reached out to me because of Gillian's references. Although Gillian retired as Director of the Anne Frank Trust UK, she remains active in the field of philanthropy which she loves.

Nicholas Zane

FOREWORD

Jews in China: A History of Struggle tells the powerful story of Jewish struggle and survival in the Middle Kingdom.

Nicholas Zane skilfully condenses centuries of historical information about four main groups of Jewish immigrants to China into this succinct, but comprehensive, chronicle. The Kaifeng Jews, who now look no different from their Chinese neighbours due to thousands of years of intermarriage and assimilation; the Baghdadi Jews, who came to Shanghai after the First Opium War and became fabulously wealthy through opium trade and real estate development; the Russian Jews, who left the Pale of Settlement for a better life in Harbin and prospered by supplying vast natural resources from Northeast China to Europe; and last but not least, the tens of thousands of German and Austrians Jews who escaped Nazi-occupied Europe and found refuge in Shanghai.

The author delves thoroughly into the long, unique history of the Kaifeng Jews, whose timeline of Sinification spans from the Han dynasty to the founding of present day China. What this depth of detail unveils is the importance of preserving the legacy and uniqueness of the Kaifeng Jews' history: they managed to sustain a culture that was unquestionably Jewish, whilst seamlessly assimilating into Chinese civilization.

The Chinese and the Jewish people have always shared a great deal in common — a respect for education, a love of entrepreneurship, and a high esteem in which culture and tradition are viewed. Today, they share even more. The book is an attentive tribute to two ancient civilizations who have, in an extraordinary fashion, managed to blend beliefs, cultures, and traditions without conflict or fear.

This book, written as an accessible read for those even with minimal prior knowledge of Chinese or Jewish history, is filled with heart-warming stories and precious photographs from the Kaifeng Jewish Memorial Center, the Shanghai Jewish Refugees Museum, and the author's own archives. All in all, Zane provides a tantalizingly view into the Jewish diaspora in China – their incredible history and legacy.

A must read.

Martina Ingrouille
Kellet School
Hong Kong, April 2019

PART I:

KAIFENG JEWS

1. City of Kaifeng

The city of Kaifeng (开封市) is located 10 kilometers south of the renowned Yellow River (黄河), the second longest river in China — second only to the Yangtze River — as well as the cradle of Chinese civilization. Covering much of the heartland of the Middle Kingdom, spanning all the way from Qinghai province (青海省) to Shandong province (山东省), the Yellow River facilitates trade on a large scale.

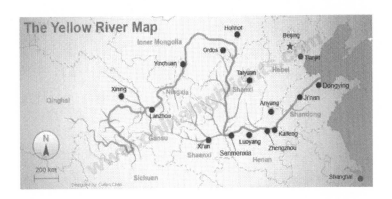

Figure 1 Chinese civilisation originated from the middle and lower basins of the Yellow River, then spread across China, into East Asia. [chinahighlights.com]

Hence, by the turn of the Song Dynasty (宋朝), Kaifeng was already a bustling hub of commerce and therefore chosen to be the capital of China. The extensive trade made Kaifeng not only the economic powerhouse of China, but arguably of the entire world, given the vastness of the Middle Kingdom at the time. The economic prosperity brought with it political stability as well as a golden age, as the city flourished in terms of arts, music, culture, and philosophy.

Although Kaifeng, in the 21st century, is relatively unheard of, especially to the western countries, rest assured that its position as the capital of Northern Song — as well as six other feudalist dynasties — has earned it a place on the shelf. Along with Beijing (北京), Xi'an (西安), Nanjing (南京), Luoyang (洛阳), and Hangzhou (杭州), Kaifeng is one of the 'six great capitals' of China.

However, Kaifeng's proximity to the Yellow River brought to it more than just prosperous civilizations; along with people and settlements the Yellow River brought to Kaifeng floods — quite frequently, in fact. Throughout China's 4,000-year history over 1,000 major floods that brought cities to their knees have been recorded, and a large fraction, albeit unknown, took place in Henan province, where Kaifeng is located.

It might be mentioned that there were in fact benefits brought to Kaifeng by the flooding, such as a need for advancements. The potential of a flood meant that governments had to become more systematic, insofar as planning defensive mechanisms to combat the floods. However, Kaifeng did still suffer much devastation, most notable being the 1642 Yellow River Flood.

In more recent history, Kaifeng has, however, become less suitable a place to house anything of large significance. The advancements in architecture has brought China out of the wood & bricks phase of short-term structures, and into the steel and concrete phase of modern skyscrapers. In the past, to rebuild houses and buildings destroyed by the Yellow River was an endeavor that was neither overly financially draining nor time-consuming; however, now, a major flood could leave a city like Kaifeng with billions of dollars' worth of destruction. Moreover, China's increased level of international maritime trade and improved railways and roads means that incentive to locate a city right by a river bank has fallen, for there are many locations much more efficient and less damage-prone.

As such, in 1954, the newly established People's Republic of China made the decision to move the provincial capital of Henan province from Kaifeng to Zhengzhou city. Subsequently, Zhengzhou became the heart of northern China's railway transportation system and an economically dominant powerhouse in many aspects. Today, Kaifeng in almost all aspects falls short to its more prosperous neighbor Zhengzhou.

Figure 2 As the capital of Henan Province, Zhengzhou now sits on main railway crossings in central China. [chinatourmap.com]

If you make the (unlikely) decision to take a trip to the once renowned city of Kaifeng, you will find a flat, smog-covered town with minimum industrial outputs. The friends you will make there will likely be in their later stages of life, as most young people in Kaifeng, seeking potential job opportunities, have left for larger cities — Beijing, Shanghai, Shenzhen, and, of course, Zhengzhou.

2. Kaifeng Jews

In 2019, a trip to the city of Kaifeng will bring you minimal joy, at best, compared with many other destinations in the once–Kingdom in the middle of the world. However, behind the lack of commotion lives quietly a remarkable community of Jews: the Jews of Kaifeng. For tens of centuries, the Jews of Kaifeng have been a part-Jewish, part-Chinese needle in a haystack of mostly pure Han Chinese citizens. This community, boasting an incredibly lineage and history, embody the merging of two ancient cultures — Chinese and Jewish — which are often thought of in isolation to one another.

The Kaifeng Jews are the descendants of Sephardic Jews who immigrated to China millenniums ago and the Han Chinese, indigenous to the Middle Kingdom. The Jews of Kaifeng, according to stone inscriptions, were made up of 70 clans (or families) when they first set foot in China; unfortunately, after nearly a hundred generations, due to numerous instances of social, political, and natural upheavals, their population has declined significantly, leaving a headcount of barely 1,000.

Figure 3 In Hebrew and Chinese, "For My House Shall Be Called a House of Prayer For All Peoples." [Nicholas Zane Archives]

During later stages of the Qing Dynasty (when the west was going through its industrial revolution) doubts rose amongst scholars over the authenticity of Kaifeng Jews' claimed Jewish heritage. Indeed, since only a fraction of the Jews in Kaifeng still adhered to Judaic principles — such as observing the Sabbath — a hint of doubt is at the very least warranted. Moreover, because generations of intermarriage and interbreeding with the indigenous Han Chinese has left the Kaifeng Jewish population, virtually, physically indistinguishable from any pure Han Chinese neighbors, disputes regarding their lineage is understandable.

In the 1980s, China under President Deng Xiaoping (邓小平) opened its doors to the west, following a 30-year period of isolation, extending from the founding of the People's Republic of China to the Cultural Revolution. Many Jews from different parts of the world began to pour into China to visit this very special community in Kaifeng. The Kaifeng Jews at this point knew very little about their purported Jewish heritage but were eager to reconnect with the roots of their forefathers. As such, following DNA tests conducted in the 1980s which came back positive and confirmed their Jewish claim, the visitors brought to the Jews of Kaifeng books on Jewish history, culture, language, and religion; they showed the Jews of Kaifeng what it 'actually' meant to be Jewish, and the more Orthodox conventions of Judaism.

Figure 4 A modern Kaifeng Jew household. [Nicholas Zane Archives]

The affirmative DNA tests also helped gain the Jews of Kaifeng the recognition of many Jewish institutions around the world, not least Shavei Israel. Shavei Israel was founded by Michael Freund who in the 1990s served a term as Prime Minister Benjamin Netanyahu's director of communications. The organization was established to locate 'Lost Tribes of Israel' and help them reconnect with their motherland — Israel. Shavei Israel, over the past decade, has helped bring 20 Jews of Kaifeng return to Israel, or in more extravagant terms 'make Aliyah.'

Figure 5 With the help of Shavei Israel, 5 young Kaifeng Jews made Aliyah — the return of diaspora Jews to Israel, in 2016. [Shavei Israel]

As the Jews of Kaifeng, however, do not strictly adhere to certain Jewish traditions — because, for instance, maintain a purely kosher diet in China is practically impossible — they are required to undergo full conversion in order to become Jews recognized by the state and in order to receive Israeli citizenship.

It should be clarified that Jews located in Beijing, Shanghai, and Hong Kong are western Jews: they are Jews who live in China. Whereas the Jews of Kaifeng are ethnic-Chinese of Jewish descent: they are Chinese-Jews and consider themselves to be the only proper community of Chinese-Jews in the world.

In a country of 1.4 billion people, it is astonishing to see this community of less than 1,000 people, living in a smog-covered city far away in central China, continuing to — at least to some degree — embrace their Jewish identity. It may be considered unfathomable that their Jewish culture and Jewish identity — amid heavy assimilation, especially in the Ming Dynasty — survived almost 2,000 years of China's turbulent history. This is indeed a story which deserves to be told and retold. Guo Yan, curator of the Kaifeng Jewish History Memorial Center, puts it perfectly: "just like Russian Jews and American Jews, Chinese Jews have their own history and it's important to remember it." [2016]

3. Identity

The completeness of the Jewish identity of the Jews of Kaifeng may be subject to debate. They no longer practice most Jewish traditions, nor do they observe most Jewish holidays, including the all-important Hanukah; they have had no rabbis for over two centuries; they have not had a synagogue or seen the congregation of Jewish communities for generations; their ancestors intermarried and followed patrilineal descent (being Jewish is matrilineal); and their features are no longer distinguishingly Jewish. And, whilst some Jewish communities consider them not Jewish — only of Jewish descent — the Jews of Kaifeng consider themselves wholeheartedly as Jews, regardless of what their critics think. It should be pointed out that the fact the Jews of Kaifeng have any idea about their Jewish heritage is quite impressive, given the many centuries that could have changed this.

Figure 6 Kaifeng Jews from the early 20th century. [Kaifeng Jewish History Memorial Center]

The Jews of Kaifeng acknowledge an underlying affinity between Chinese and Jewish thinking and believe it has helped with their integration into society. Even if the Chinese lack a firm concept of a monotheistic supreme deity, the two shares strikingly many similar values — to name a few — both are incredibly competitive, have a strong entrepreneurial mindset, place a relatively large importance on education, and emphasis respect of the elderly. Indeed, the stone inscription tablets, which used to be kept in the courtyard of the Kaifeng Synagogue, consistently referred to the similar principles that often brought together Confucianism and Judaism.

Most important perhaps on the list of the few Jewish values that survived was the emphasis of respecting the elderly —

filial piety and 'honor thy father and thy mother'. The Kaifeng Jews, as a means to honor the elderly — even if they have past away — held tight to any cultural heritages that were passed down to them. They, moreover, stayed true to their ancestors by never converting the Taoism and Buddhism — however compelling it may be in dynastical China; and, by living in close proximity to their synagogue. The Jews of Kaifeng think of themselves are proudly Chinese, and, at the same time, authentically Jewish.

The fact that Jews in Kaifeng do not practice some elements of Judaism is due to the practical component. For instance, working on the Shabbat is necessary and kosher salt is virtually unobtainable in China.

Figure 7 Israeli flag in a modern Kaifeng Jew's household. [Nicholas Zane Archives]

Michael Freund of Shavei Israel observed, "Even though their knowledge of Judaism was very low, they still retained great pride that their ancestors were Jews; it was something they nourished and passed down to later generations." [2016]

4. Assimilation

In China, the Jews of Kaifeng found a civilization untouched by Biblical religions of Christianity, Judaism, and Islam. Where the Jews may have had a conflict of interest in the interpretation of the Old Testament with the Christians, they had no such issues with the Chinese. As such, the Jews in Kaifeng were never singled out as a group in a negative sense. China was a haven in which they could live freely, and anti-Semitism was a concept they need not worry about.

During their integration into the vast Middle Kingdom, the Kaifeng Jews not only faced no troubles, they were in fact viewed highly, as exemplary citizens for attaining a disproportionately high number of positions as civil servants through Chinese Imperial Examinations (more on this in the Ming Dynasty chapter). The community took great pride in this and therefore publicly displayed any gifts received from emperors over many centuries.

The non-religious aspect of the Jews' life came to be very similar to that of the Chinese, especially after the Ming

Dynasty. They adopted the Chinese language (only rabbis and Jewish scholars continued to study Hebrew, although this ended in 1810 when the last rabbi past away), cuisine (apart from pork and some other non-kosher dishes), clothing, and secular education. In the Qing Dynasty, Jewish men began to wear pigtails, when it became new custom following a decree passed by Qing conquerors.

Figure 8 Kaifeng Jews during the Qing Dynasty. [Kaifeng Jewish History Memorial Center]

Their religious traditions were also largely influenced by local norms. From their very early days in China, the Jews of Kaifeng added great Chinese classics to the studying of Hebrew and the Torah. Their most beloved synagogue, when constructed in the 12th century, followed Judaic law insofar as the lack of idols and paintings on the walls (with exceptions later explained), but different in that the exterior of the synagogue was purely oriental. Indeed, a perfect example of Jews maintaining the integrity of their religion while adapting to the local surroundings this was.

Figure 9 A model of the original Kaifeng synagogue, exhibiting Chinese temple architectural style on the exterior. [Nicholas Zane Archives]

The Chinese influence was by no means a decisive force in shaping the religious experience of Jews in Kaifeng, it supplemented Jewish tradition instead by, for instance, adding in the Chinese practice of offering food and drinks, and burning incense to deceased friends and relatives.

However, in many other regards, the Jews of Kaifeng did indeed blend into their surroundings and gradually became more like their Han neighbours than their predecessors. The assimilation of the Kaifeng Jews can arguably have been excessively extreme to a degree which can be categorised as fatal to the existence of Judaism in China.

"For the student of Jewish culture, Kaifeng is the opposite of the usual story of survival in the face of persecution," said Dr Karen Wilson, Research Fellow at the UCLA Center for Jewish Studies, "Kaifeng is the rare example of a Jewish community coexisting happily with a broader culture that accepted it." [1986]

5. Compromise

The Jews of Kaifeng oftentimes willingly took upon Chinese practices; however, oftentimes, there would be a conflict of interest between Chinese and Jewish culture, which would force the Jews of Kaifeng into compromise, if the Chinese custom was backed by law.

According to the Torah, if a married man died without a child, his brother was obliged to marry his widow. The surviving brother would take over the estate of the deceased brother. The offspring of this union would take on the name of the deceased brother. This practice ensured the continuity of the deceased brother's legacy, kept the family together and offered protection to the widow. However, levirate marriage was illegal under Chinese imperial law and the Jews of Kaifeng had to put this practice to a halt.

Certain Chinese emperors also demanded that their portraits be hung on the walls of every place of worship. This was clearly against Judaic teachings. The Jews had no choice but to put portraits of emperors on the entrance of synagogue;

however, on top of the portraits, they always wrote in Hebrew the holy prayer of Shema Yisrael which translates to "Hear, O Israel: The Lord our God, the Lord is one." To the Jews, this meant God was above all the Chinese emperors.

6. Perseverance

The Jews of Kaifeng never faced the issue of anti-Semitism as did their western counterparts, nor was the issue of malicious pressure from above an issue; however, the Jews of Kaifeng had to persevere a great deal, as implicit forces waged battle against the community.

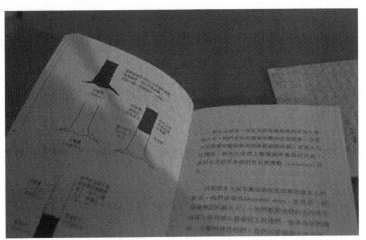

Figure 10 Booklet about Judaism —— in Chinese —— treasured by the modern day Kaifeng Jews. [Nicholas Zane Archives]

Considering their low head count, the extended period of isolation from the outside world, and the countless upheavals over two thousand years of Chinese history, it is indeed remarkable that this tiny outpost of Judaism, amidst the vast Middle Kingdom, still exists. Their seamless integration into the Chinese society, together with the inclusiveness of China's own religions, allowed them to develop a unique theology that differentiated themselves from China and the west. The stone tablets their ancestors left behind illustrated the great emphasis placed on drawing a parallelism between Judaism and Confucianism.

For centuries, in a location far away from their homeland, they followed a lifestyle that was quite similar to that of their counterparts elsewhere in the world. They had their own synagogue, observed Sabbath, took ritual baths, and maintained cemeteries. They kept a slaughterhouse and followed a kosher diet. They circumcised their sons, taught their young the Hebrew language and scripture, and gave their new-borns Hebrew names as well as local names. They ensured the moral parameters by which they conducted their lives fell within the guideline of the Torah. In an environment of multiple religious believes, they stayed faithful to their one and only God. They never forgot to pray westwards, in the direction of Jerusalem.

In 1801, their last rabbi passed away. In 1854, their synagogue disappeared under the Yellow River flood. They lost both a spiritual leader and a physical space of worship. They had no Chinese translation of the scripture and no one in the community could read Hebrew. With no more tangible attachment to their heritage, many scholars predicted the eventual extinction of this Sino-Judaic civilisation.

The community's unwavering loyalty to their Jewish origin, family lineage, ancestral worship and oral history ensured they held on tight and passed down all Judaic beliefs and practices they knew. Over time, however, stories fragmented and many customs were lost. Perhaps even without knowing the reason, they stuck to the custom of avoiding pork and retained their own version of "Jewish" identity.

In terms of clothing, Kaifeng Jews continued to wear blue kippahs to distinguish themselves from the Muslims in China who wore white headgears. Although Han Chinese were often confused, mistook them to be a sub-sect of Islam and called them "the Muslims with Blue Caps (蓝帽回)", the Kaifeng Jews continued this tradition and preserved their unique identity.

Rabbi Anson Laytner, former president of the Sino-Judaic Institute and retired Judaic studies professor at Seattle University, notably stated, "like other people, I was fascinated by their story of survival and impressed by their commitment to their Jewish identity even when they only had memories to keep that identity alive." [2018]

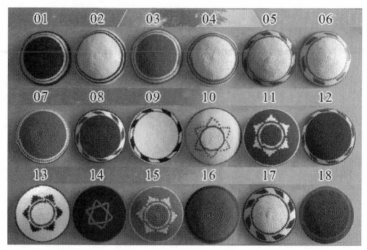

Figure 11 Blue kippahs that distinguished the Jews from the Muslims in China.
[taobao.com]

PART II

IMPERIAL CHINA

7. 汉朝 Han Dynasty (206 BC–220)

7.1

Alexander the Great (336–323 BC)

Alexander III of Macedon, better known as Alexander the Great, was the king of the ancient Greek kingdom of Macedon at its peak. He was tutored by the renowned philosopher Aristotle until he was 16. Then starting from the age of 20, Alexander the Great built and ruled one of the largest empires of the ancient world, stretching from Greece to north western India. Over twenty cities bore his name, most notably Alexandria in Egypt. His reign helped to spread Greek culture eastward which resulted in a brand new Hellenistic civilisation.

Figure 12 Alexander the Great. [British Museum]

Alexander the Great took over Jerusalem in 331 BC and made it the capital of the then Greek province of Judaea. He was known for his tolerance of the people he conquered.

During his reign, Jerusalem flourished into an important commercial centre, Jews lived and traded prosperously throughout the land. When Jews were living away from their capital, they continued to learn Hebrew language and customs, and paid a special tax for the up keeping of the Jerusalem Temple.

In 323 BC, Alexander the Great, at the young age of 33, fell violently ill. As he had no heir, he was asked on his death bed, whom he would like to bequeath his empire. He replied with a simple "to the strongest" hoping the strongest man would be able to hold together and continue to expand his kingdom.

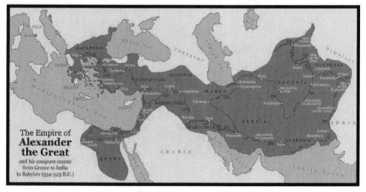

Figure 13 [reddit.com]

Alexander the Great's wish, however, did not come true. The years following his death were marked by several major civil wars fought amongst his generals which tore apart his empire. Judaea fell into the hands of the Egyptians in what would become the Ptolemaic Dynasty (305 BC–30 BC). Judaea remained free from major upheavals for most of the third century BC. In 198 BC, it was taken over by King Antiochus III of the Seleucid Empire. This was a man who would wreak havoc upon Jerusalem and make life for Jews a perpetual nightmare.

7.2

Seleucid Empire (312–63 BC)

The Seleucid Empire, founded by one of Alexander's leading generals — Seleucus I Nicator — was a Greek Hellenistic state. It was arguably the largest successor states to Alexander's Macedonian Empire, with a population of 50–60 million people, comprised of tens of different ethnicities.

The rulers built large Greek cities throughout its conquered land, and encouraged Greeks to migrate to these cities. They followed the Greek system of government by having assemblies, councils and elected magistrates.

They tried to assimilate the locals, forcing them to adopt Greek philosophical and religious thoughts. There was also a distinct hierarchy in the society where people of Greek ancestry were generally ranked higher than the natives.

Over time, many of the cities, especially those located far away from the capital, began to break away from the heart of the empire.

7.3

Antiochus III (222 BC–187 BC)

Antiochus III, the sixth emperor of the Seleucid Empire (also known as Antiochus the Great), attempting to reproduce the conquests of Alexander the Great, tried to take back lost provinces and restore the greatness of the empire.

Figure 14 Antiochus III. [Carole Raddato, Louvre]

He fought the Ptolemaic Kingdom, and failed in conquering Egypt in 217 BC, but was successful in annexing Judaea in 199 BC. Josephus recorded him as friendly towards the Jews of Jerusalem and recognized their loyalty to him. He lowered taxes, provided funding to the Temple and allowed the Jews to live "according to the law of their forefathers."

7.4

Antiochus IV (175 BC–164 BC)

As a son and potential successor of Antiochus III, Antiochus IV lived part of his early years as a political hostage to the Roman Republic. He was allowed to return home when his brother succeeded his father to the throne and his nephew was taken as a political hostage in his stead. In 175 BC, Antiochus IV seized the throne for himself.

Figure 15 Antiochus IV. [José Luiz Bernardes Ribeiro, Altes Museum]

Antiochus IV held a different view towards the people in the Seleucid Empire. He insisted that all people under his rule conformed to the Greek way of living, including religious rituals and worship. He believed in a more aggressive approach based on a stronger army. He wanted a much faster Hellenization process, accompanied by a ruthless application of force.

Wanting to surpass his father, and unite the Seleucid and Ptolemaic kingdoms into one super-empire, Antiochus in 170 BC conquered all of Egypt except Alexandra. In 168 BC, he went to Egypt again to capture Alexandria but was stopped by Rome.

While he was away, two fractions of Jerusalem Jews, Hellenised Jews and traditional Jews, started to fight against each other. Frustrated by his defeat in Egypt and the thought of a revolt in Judaea, he ruthlessly attacked Jerusalem, raided the Temple, and executed thousands of Jews.

According to 2 Maccabees 5:11–14, "He ordered his soldiers to cut down without mercy those whom they met and to slay those who took refuge in their houses. There was a massacre of young and old, killing of women and children, a slaughter of virgins and infants. In the space of three days, eighty thousand were lost, forty thousand meeting a violent death, and the same number being sold into slavery."

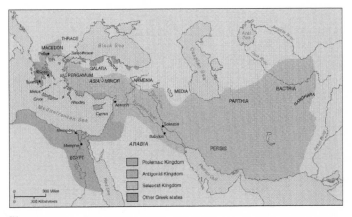

The Hellenistic Kingdoms. Alexander's generals split his empire among themselves, creating three major kingdoms sharing a common Greek culture.

Figure 16 [sites.psu.edu]

Subsequently, a statue of Zeus, with a face made to look like Antiochus IV's was constructed in the Holy of Holies of the Temple and Judaism was outlawed.

- Assemble for Jewish prayers was illegal
- Observance of Sabbath was illegal
- Possession of scriptures was illegal
- Circumcision was illegal
- Dietary laws were illegal
- Worship of Yahweh was illegal
- Pagan worship and pagan sacrifices were mandated

Antiochus IV called himself Antiochus Epiphanes or Antiochus the Magnificent, but the Jews, and history, called him Antiochus Epimames or Antiochus the Madman.

7.5

汉朝 Han Dynasty (206 BC–200)

During this time, many Jews escaped Judaea in order to continue living the Jewish way of life. Some of them eventually landed themselves in the Middle Kingdom — China. The descendants of these people would not have heard about what happened regarding the subsequent revolts and the celebration of Hanukah until 1605 AD, when a Chinese Jew named Ai Tian met Matteo Ricci in Beijing.

Far away in the east, China was experiencing an age of significant economic prosperity under the Han Dynasty (206 BC–220); many refer to this period as one of China's most significant Gold Ages. The legacy of this dynasty is clear: To this day, China's main ethnic group is called "Han Chinese", and the language "Han language".

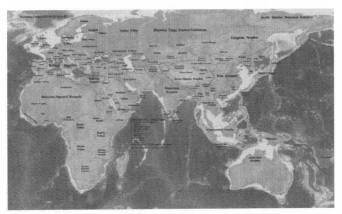

Figure 17 Map of the Eastern Hemisphere during second century BC. [Thomas Lessman]

It must be pointed out that there is in fact no decisive evidence which supports the fact that the Jews arrived in China by the Han Dynasty; however, this approach is preferred by some historians because it fits into the narrative which is elaborated on in the Ming Dynasty section of the book. The stone tablet of 1512, which now resides in the Kaifeng Municipal Museum, mentioned the Jews first came to china during Zhou Dynasty (1046–256 BC) via India.

Alternative perspectives argue that either the Jews did not leave to China until the Tang Dynasty, during which Jewish merchants came to the Middle Kingdom; or, the Jews left Judea during the Han Dynasty and travelled eastwards to India, settling in the Ganges Valley before arriving in China.

Emperor Han Wudi (汉武帝刘彻, 141–87 BC) was the emperor of China at the time. He officially endorsed Confucianism during his reign: this then fused into Chinese education, culture, politics and way of living for millenniums to come. This policy endured until the fall of China's last dynasty — the Qing Dynasty, in 1911.

Emperor Han Wudi also launched several military campaigns against the Xiongnu (匈 奴), a nomadic confederation along China's western border. The ultimate Han victory expanded Han sovereignty into the Tarim Basin of Central Asia and helped establish a vast trade network — which came to be known as the Silk Road — reaching as far as the Mediterranean world. Some scholars believe this to be the route by which the Jews travelled to reach China.

Figure 18 Emperor Han Wudi (汉武帝刘彻, 141–87 BC). [bestchinanews.com]

7.6

Maccabean Revolt & Hanukkah

Whilst the conflict caused a diaspora which urged many Jews to move eastwards, some Jews remained in Jerusalem and joined Judas Maccabeus in his rebellion. The rebels employed guerrilla warfare, likely a decisive tactic which helped to ultimately bring about the defeat of Antiochus IV and his large army. By 165 BC, the Jewish revolutionaries regained control of Jerusalem.

Indeed, the Jews feasted over their victory for eight days straight, a celebration which would soon come to be known as Hanukah.

The legacy of the war for the Seleucid Empire was nowhere near as long lasting, as it was a first step in the wrong direction for the empire, which was ultimately overthrown in 63 BC by Roman General Pompey.

Figure 19 A collection of Menorahs in a modern Kaifeng Jew's home.[Nicholas Zane Archives]

8. 唐朝 Tang Dynasty (618–907)

Figure 20 [Minneapolis Institute of Arts]

China experienced an unprecedented Golden Age during the Tang Dynasty, a period which saw the Middle Kingdom flourish in all aspects: philosophy, art, music, literature. It was, moreover, a period of liberalism, one which saw women with a greater degree of personal freedom than before, for instance, in terms of more revealing clothing. A nation at its top shape economically and socially, China became increasingly attractive to foreigners and merchants who would begin to, on a larger scale, use the Silk Road as a means of trading with the vast Middle Kingdom. Indeed, some historians think that it was during this dynasty that Jewish merchants first entered China and began to settle down, forming the foundation of the Chinese-Jews.

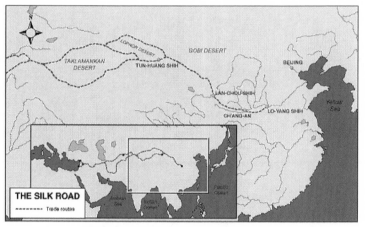

Figure 21 [Minneapolis Institute of Arts]

8.1

Earliest Evidence of Jews in China

The earliest evidence of Jews' existence in China dates back to the year 718, in a business letter written in Judaeo-Persian language that was found in Dandan Oilik (丹丹乌里克). Dandan Oilik, also called "the houses of ivory," was an important outpost along the Silk Road. It is located in the Taklamakan desert (塔克拉玛干沙漠), in today's Xinjiang Province (新疆省). The letter was written on paper. The author of the letter, a Persian-speaking Jew, wrote to a fellow Jew asking him to help him to sell some inferior grade sheep. Indeed, the fact that paper was used is evidence of Jews in China because at the time paper was a commodity which could only be found in the Middle Kingdom.

More evidence of Jews in China during this period comes from the caves of Dunhuang (敦煌), which is in today's Gansu Province (甘肃省). Contained in the caves, stretched over 25 kilometres, are 492 temples which contain a collection of priceless manuscripts and artworks which have been uncovered in the past few centuries. This collection notably contained a penitential prayer from the Psalms written in Hebrew.

The earliest historical writings that referenced the existence of Jews in China were by Abu Zayd Hasan of Siraf, an Arab explorer. Hasan wrote about a rebellion in 878 lead by

Huang Chao (黄巢), that severally weakened the Tang Dynasty government. When Huang captured the city of Guangzhou (广州), his army killed 120,000 foreign residents; and, amongst them, Jews.

Figure 22 Judaeo-Persian manuscript founded in Dandan Oilik , dated to year 718. [Public Domain]

9. 北宋 Northern Song Dynasty (960–1127)

Figure 23 [Minneapolis Institute of Arts]

The Northern Song Dynasty was a time during which Chinese culture was granted large importance but military was given little emphasis. The relatively weak military of the Northern Song was unable to properly keep the Silk Road in check so that merchants could travel safely; with the predominant land route losing traction, trading between China and Central Asia took place mostly on sea routes, via the Indian Ocean, reaching China's Southern seaports such as Ningbo (宁波).

Figure 24 First Emperor of the Song Dynasty — Emperor Song Taizu (宋太祖赵匡胤, 960–976). [Public Domain]

While Tang had its capital in Xi'an which was at the terminus of the Silk Road, the Song government moved its capital 550 kilometres eastward, to the city of Kaifeng due to its geographical proximity to the Yellow River. The Grand Canal (大运河) helped to transport goods from China's Southern seaports to Kaifeng. Since China's main rice fields and silk production facilities were all in the South, the canal played a significant role in facilitating domestic trade and tax collection. Soon, Kaifeng flourished. Kaifeng, being the capital of China, could be argued to have been the most important city in the world at the time, given the immenseness of the Chinese empire.

Figure 25 Parts of the Qingming Shanghe Tu (清明上河图), a Song Dynasty artwork depicting life in the bustling city of Kaifeng. It is the most renowned of all Chinese paintings, holding the status equivalent to the Mona Lisa of the West in China. [Public Domain]

The political atmosphere in the west during this period was dominated by the Christian Crusades, targeted at recovering the Holy Land from the Muslims. When the Crusaders recaptured Jerusalem in 1099, they ruthlessly slaughtered Muslim residents; Jewish communities in the vicinity were caught in the commotion and had a choice between surrendering and facing their untimely death. Many Jews fled instead and made their way to China.

During the early part of the Song Dynasty, the conservative elite of China wore clothes made of silk; however, silk was extremely difficult to produce and expensive — especially given the demand for silk from aboard — and therefore inaccessible to a majority of Chinese citizens. The less wealthy wore clothing made of hemp, a rough fabric, particularly uncomfortable during the summer, due to its insulating properties. The use of cotton gained traction during this dynasty, as it combined the comfortable properties of silk and the easy production of hemp.

Since many Jewish merchants at the time specialised in trading cotton produced in India and Pakistan, plenty of traders settled down in China while bringing cotton to the far east, thus becoming another wave of Jewish immigrants arriving in China. Indeed, given that Kaifeng was the capital of China at the time, most of the traders would end up finding their way there.

In 998, the Kaifeng Jews presented Emperor Song Zhenzhong (宋真宗赵德昌, 997–1022) a multi-hued cotton as a tribute. Emperor Zhenzhong was greatly pleased and in response bestowed 12 blessed words to the entire Kaifeng Jewish community — 归我中夏，遵守祖风，留遗汴梁 (Be a part of our country, practice your traditions, and live in Kaifeng).

10. 大金 Great Jin Dynasty (1115–1234)

Figure 26 [museocineseparma.org]

The Great Jin Dynasty was founded by the descendants of Jurchen people (女真人) who lived in the region of Manchuria. Over the course of their rule, the Jurchens adapted Chinese customs and revived Confucianism. They married Han Chinese, studied Chinese classics and wrote Chinese poetry.

Around the end of the 11th century, Chinese peasants frequently produced counterfeit money. Naturally, in order to avert economic issues the Northern Song government introduced a currency that was difficult to forge — a task harder than it sounds — and they were very successful in doing so.

Figure 27 Jin coins. [Jean-Michel Moullec from Vern sur Seiche, France]

However, this solution was only as long-lasting as its enforcers — as Jin replaced the Northern Song, counterfeits skyrocketed at an unprecedented rate, resulting in hyperinflation and social unrest. The Jews were traditionally known for their financial expertise, the Jin government therefore sought their assistance in trying to combat the nation's turmoil.

The Jews in Kaifeng were of major help, and the economic crisis soon came to an end.

10.1

Kaifeng Synagogue of 1163

As an act of gratitude, in 1163, the Jin government granted the Jews in Kaifeng a plot of land and subsidised the construction of the Kaifeng synagogue. The assigned land was bounded by the Teaching Torah Lane North (北教经胡同) and Teaching Torah Lane South (南教经胡同). The synagogue was accompanied by sukkah, study area, ritual bath, large kitchen and kosher butchering facility. Scholars believed the original congregation probably had 500 people, composed of 70 clans (or families).

Figure 28 Teaching Torah Lane, still in use today. [Nicholas Zane Archive]

While the Kaifeng Jews embraced many elements of Chinese culture, they guarded hard their own faith. The synagogue had a traditional Chinese architecture on the outside but it differed from other places of worship in China on the inside — there were no idols of any form. Generations of Jewish children studied Hebrew and Torah here. The facility also allowed the Jews to follow a kosher diet. The Chinese called them "the Religion that Plucks Out the Sinews (挑筋教)" in reference to their custom of removing thigh muscle from Kosher meat.

Over the next 700 years, this synagogue was destroyed and rebuilt at least nine times. They had a rabbi until 1810.

The significance of the synagogue and Jin Dynasty's favourable policies could not be understated, for soon came the golden age for the Chinese-Jewish community, which saw their population risen above 5000.

11. 元朝 Yuan Dynasty (1271–1368)

Figure 29 [Minneapolis Institute of Arts]

Yuan Dynasty, founded by Kublai Khan (元世祖忽必烈), was a relatively friendly time for the Kaifeng Jews. No different from anywhere else in the Mongolian Empire, Kaifeng inhabitants were granted full freedom of religion.

Figure 30 Kublai Khan (元世祖忽必烈, 1215–1294), founder of the Yuan Dynasty, was the grandson of Genghis Khan. [Public Domain]

The Mongolians removed the caste system which gave the ethnic Han Chinese a decisive advantage in society and implemented their own legislation which would undermine the Han Chinese. Indeed, the new Mongolian caste system divided the population into four ranks:

I.   Mongolians (蒙古人)

II.   Semu (色目人) — Descendants of people from Central and West Asia

III. Northern Han Chinese (汉人) — People from the Great Jin Dynasty

IV.   Southern Han Chinese (南人) — People from the Southern Song Dynasty

With higher nose bridges and lighter hair and eye colour, the Jews of Kaifeng were quite visibly non-Han Chinese and therefore placed into the Semu class, second only to the ruling Mongolians themselves.

The Mongols distrusted the Han. They ended the civil service examination system that has been used in China for centuries to select government officials. And, in its stead, placed non-Han Chinese, including Jews, into strategic positions in government. The Jews, fluent in Chinese language and familiar with both western and Chinese culture, helped the ruling Mongols in running the country.

However, in 1280 the Mongols banned all Jewish and Muslim ritual slaughters because the Yuan Emperor decided that if pork was good enough for him it should be good enough for any of his subjects.

12. 明朝 Ming Dynasty (1368–1644)

Figure 31 [Minneapolis Institute of Arts]

By 1368 the Han Chinese regained control of the Middle
Kingdom and expelled the Mongolians. Domestically, there
was a strong revival of Confucianism and Chinese traditions;
civil service examination was back in full swing. Living under
the rule of foreigners cultured sceptical view of outsiders

amongst the Han Chinese. As such, the Han Chinese rulers sealed the borders of China. For the next 200 years, the Jews of Kaifeng lost all contact with the rest of the world.

12.1

Religious Studies vs Secular Duties

During this dynasty, the Jews were active participants and extremely productive members of Chinese society. Some continued to be merchants, a profitable but less respected profession, whilst a disproportionately large number of them, in fact, passed the Imperial Examination and gained high ranking positions as civil servants.

Figure 32 Analects by Confucius, a must read for the Civil Service Examination.
[Bjoertvedt, Östasiatiska Museet, Stockholm]

As these great Jewish minds thoroughly studied Chinese classics in order to pass the Imperial Examinations, they had to sacrifice time which could otherwise be spent on learning the teachings of their own culture: stories of Abraham and

Moses. In essence, they had to abandon the study of who they were in order to succeed in the secular world.

12.2

Intermarriage

Emperor HongWu (洪武帝朱元璋), the first emperor of the dynasty, assumed that role after leading a peasant revolution against the Mongolians of the Yuan Dynasty. He was the one who closed the borders of China out of distrust for outsiders.

Within China, he wanted to ensure social harmony amongst its people, so he introduced an intermarriage act, which required ethnic minorities to marry outside of their own communities.

Figure 33 Emperor Hongwu (洪武帝朱元璋) decreed the intermarriage law during his 5th year on the throne. [Public Domain]

71

As such, Jewish men began to marry Chinese women. Because of the patriarchal nature of China, women, after they were married, were to completely integrate into their husband's family and traditions and forget about their own. Thus, it can be speculated, that these families continued to maintain a primarily Jewish lifestyle.

However, this led to the dilution of Judaism on a large scale. Firstly, Judaism follows a matrilineal descent. In the strictest sense, therefore, all of these children were not technically Jewish. Secondly, since men were the breadwinners of the family, the Jewish fathers were out working most of the time, whilst the Chinese mothers were the ones raising the children. Because the mothers, themselves, were Chinese, they did not have the knowledge to teach their children about Judaism, even if they wanted to. And most of the time, they did not.

The reason parents were reluctant was because of the social structure of China, which placed a large emphasis on social standing. Chinese society was divided into four groups (albeit not in the same way as it was in the Yuan Dynasty). At the bottom was the lower class which consisted of merchants. Then, came craftsmen. Then, were the humble agricultural laborers. At the very top, were the civil servants.

There was a degree of social mobility in China; to become a civil servant, at the very pinnacle of society, one had to pass a series of Imperial Examinations, which tested knowledge of Chinese teachings and literature — such as the writings of Confusions and other prominent philosophers and writers.

Therefore, even if the Chinese mothers knew about Judaism perfectly, and could recite the Torah, this kind of teaching would still be secondary because the only thing that would benefit their children, and guarantee them a prosperous life, was if they learnt about Confucius — not Moses — and passed the Imperial Exams.

12.3

Chinese Last Names

In 1421, Emperor Yongle (永乐大帝朱棣, 1402–1424) conferred the surname Zhao (赵) to a Jewish physician. In order to fully embrace this group of people who have been exemplary citizens and make them feel more at home on this foreign land, Emperor Yongle eventually granted all Jews in China one of eight Chinese surnames — Ai, Gao, Jin, Li, Shi, Zhang (two Chinese characters — both 张 and 章), and Zhao. Three of these names, Jin (金), Shi (石) and Li (李) are believed to be equivalent of common Jewish names in the west: Gold, Stone and Levi, respectively.

Because China followed the paternal lineage, the descendants of Kaifeng Jews today almost exclusively have these eight surnames.

This significant honour and landmark event served as a turning point in the complete acceptance of Jews into the mainstream Chinese society. From this juncture forward, the Jews participated actively in the civil service examinations and served in high ranking civil service positions at significantly higher proportion compared to the size of their population.

Figure 34 Emperor Yongle (永乐大帝朱棣). [Public Domain]

However, Emperor Yongle's goodwill — the replacement of Hebrew surnames with Chinese ones, made it even more difficult to distinguish the Chinese-Jews from the Han-Chinese.

12.4

Stone Tablets of 1489 & 1512

The stories of the Kaifeng Jews were mainly captured on three stone tablets, that of 1489, 1512 and 1663 (For more, see Qing Dynasty.)

At five feet tall and five inches thick, the 1489 stone tablet was the oldest and most comprehensive, containing about 1,800 inscribed Chinese characters.

It told the biblical stories of Abraham, Moses, Ezra and the origin of Judaism; it mentioned the Judaic essence of praying, fasting, and repentance; it compared Judaism with the three main Chinese religions — Buddhism, Confucianism and Taoism; it explained the basic concepts of Judaism within the context of Chinese culture and understanding; it stated that Jews immigrated to China from India during the Han Dynasty; it cited the names of 70 Jews with Chinese surnames; it commemorated the construction of the synagogue in 1163; and it praised family ancestors who served in the Imperial Court and military.

More specifically, it mentioned in 1421 Ming Emperor Yongle (永乐大帝朱棣, 1402–1424) conferred the surname Zhao (赵) to a Jewish physician named An Cheng. It also described the 12 blessed words bestowed on them by Song Emperor Zhengzong（宋真宗赵德昌，997–1022),

welcoming them to settle in Kaifeng — 归我中夏，遵守祖风，留遗汴梁 (Be a part of our country, practice your traditions, and live in Kaifeng).

The stone tablet was erected to commemorate the reconstruction of the synagogue after the flood of 1461.

Figure 35 This stone tablet now resides in the Kaifeng Municipal Museum. [Kaifeng Jewish History Memorial Center]

The 1512 stone tablet had about 1,000 Chinese characters inscribed on it. It provided information about the daily life of Jews. It included details about Jewish religious practices and stated that Judaism could not exist without the Torah; it placed heavy emphasis on the parallelism between Judaism and Confucianism; it talked about the Jews first came to china during Zhou Dynasty (1046–256 BC) via India; it mentioned other Jewish communities in China and that they had already established contact with each other; it stressed loyalty from Kaifeng Jewish community to the Chinese Imperial Court, and that the Jews had served as merchants, officials and soldiers.

Both of these tablets now reside in the Kaifeng Municipal Museum.

12.5

"Discovery" of Kaifeng Jews

Matteo Ricci

Matteo Ricci was born in 1552. At the age of 19, he joined the Society of Jesus, also known as the Jesuits. On top of the three traditional vows to the Catholic Church — poverty, chastity and obedience — the Jesuits took on a fourth vow: to go wherever in the world the Pope may send them. Jesuits placed heavy emphasis on education and scholarship. Thus, as part of his training, Ricci learned mathematics, cosmology and astronomy, as well as theology and philosophy.

This was the time of Counter-Reformation in the west. The Catholic church wanted to evangelise the world and China, with a population about that of entire Europe back then, was a huge part of the project.

In 1582, at the age of 30, Ricci arrived in Macau, a then Portuguese colony, and focused his study on Chinese language and culture. Two years later, Ricci created the first European-style map in Chinese, referred to as the Great Map of Ten Thousand Countries (万国图) by the locals. It showed China's geographical location in the world, and for the first time, opened China's eyes to the world.

Ricci also compiled the Portuguese-Chinese dictionary, the very first dictionary that linked Chinese characters to Latin alphabets.

Ricci's expertise in astronomy, particularly his ability to predict the solar eclipses, impressed the Imperial Court. In 1601, he was invited by Ming Emperor Wanlin (万历帝朱翊钧) to Beijing and became the first Westerner allowed to enter the Forbidden City. While in Beijing, he founded the Cathedral of the Immaculate Conception (圣母无染原罪堂, Or 宣武门天主堂, or 南堂), the oldest Catholic church in Beijing which still stands today.

Figure 36 Founded by Matteo Ricci in 1605, the Cathedral of the Immaculate Conception is the oldest Catholic Church in Beijing. [Nicholas Zane Archives]

Ricci completely embraced a Chinese lifestyle. He mastered written as well as classical Chinese, and lived and dressed like any mandarin on the street. Ricci believed the best way to get close to people, especially those of authority and influence, was by interesting them with the latest scientific discoveries from Europe. Thus, all the knowledge and wisdom he acquired from a faraway land, he shared them enthusiastically and freely. As a learned European gentleman, Ricci was charming, personable, and exceptionally well liked by the locals.

Figure 37 Commemorating the 400th anniversary of Matteo Ricci's death, a musical production depicting the life of Matteo Ricci was performed at the Hong Kong Cultural Centre. [Nicholas Zane Archives]

Ricci believed that it would be more effective to use written words, rather than pure speeches to get his message across to the well-learned Confucian scholars, for they held a strong love for reading. Ricci translated a significant portion of Christian text to Chinese which made Christianity more accessible to the locals.

Ricci reasoned that details of Christianity should not be unveiled in one go for it would be extremely difficult for the potentials converts to accept. He disclosed information very little at a time, made sure receivers understood before moving forward.

He held back from emphasising the most difficult parts — crucifixion, resurrection and the concept of the divine trinity. Instead, he focused on mother Mary and baby Jesus.

Ricci postulated that telling people what they knew was completely wrong was not a strategic way to engage an audience and that it was important to draw a parallelism between Christianity and the local culture.

He adapted the Chinese concept of "lord of heaven (天主)" as the diving entity to be worshipped, a terminology still used today by the Chinese in referring to Catholicism and Catholic God. Ricci also allowed for ancestor worshipping because it was such a dominant part of the native tradition.

Figure 38 Statue of Matteo Ricci at the Cathedral of Immaculate Conception, Beijing.
[Nicholas Zane Archives]

Ricci respected that different regions had different values. He completely embraced and endorsed the local culture while he evangelised. In many ways, he was more successful than the other missionaries who attempted to convert the Chinese by applying the same methodology used in the new world.

Today, Ricci is remembered as the first Christian missionary in China. He is revered for his extensive knowledge and love of learning; he is celebrated for his humility in understanding and accepting the Chinese culture; he is honoured as a legendary figure in the history of cultural exchange between China and the west. His legacy is taught in many classrooms and his name decorates some of the most significant landmarks in the region.

Figure 39 Ricci Hall (利玛窦宿舍), founded in 1929 by the Society of Jesus in memory of Matteo Ricci, is an all-boys residence hall at the University of Hong Kong. [Nicholas Zane Archives]

Ai Tian

In Ricci's book, *De Christiana expeditione apud Sinas*, he recorded that in 1605, he was visited by a Kaifeng Jew named Ai Tian.

Ai Tian had already passed the civil service examination and was in Beijing to secure a position in the Imperial Court. He heard there was a group of foreigners in town who were monotheists but were not Muslims. Although Han-Chinese found it hard to distinguish between Jews and Muslims, for neither of them ate pork, Ai Tian knew better. Since he had never heard of Christianity before, he was certain this group of foreigners were followers of Judaic faith. Ai Tian arranged to meet them.

Ai Tian was excited as the Kaifeng Jews had not had any interaction with the outside world, much less those of their own faith, for over 200 years. Ricci was equally excited. He learned Christianity had entered China long ago, perhaps as early as the 7th century, but he had not managed to locate any of their descendants. Ricci was sure he was about to finally meet a Christian in China. He invited Ai Tian to the Jesuit mission house.

In the mission house, there was a picture of Mary, with baby Jesus on one side and John the Baptist on the other. Ricci placed the image there in order to served two purposes. One was for his own worship, the other as a conversation starter with his guests — when the visitors saw the portrait, they would ask who were the people in the drawing, Ricci would then be able to very naturally share the Bible stories and evangelise.

When Ai Tian saw the picture, he thought they represented Rebecca with her two sons, Jacob and Esau. When Ricci bowed and worshipped them, Ai Tian stated that he did not worship images although he did follow as a gesture of politeness and as an act of showing respect for his ancestors.

Figure 40 Matteo Ricci. [Public Domain]

In the room, there was also a picture of the four Evangelists — Matthew, Mark, Luke and John. Ai Tian inquired if there should be 12 people in this image instead. Ricci answered yes, thinking Ai Tian must have meant the 12 apostles. When Ai Tian pressed further, saying since there were only four men here, what happened to the other eights sons of Jacob, Ricci couldn't help but finally admit to the fact that his visitor was speaking completely in the context of the Old Testament, and that he was not a Chinese Christians, but a Chinese Jew. Ai Tian told Ricci there was an entire community of Jews in Kaifeng, and that they even had their own synagogue(礼拜寺), rabbi, and Torah scrolls.

When Ai Tian went back to Kaifeng, Ricci sent Jesuits with him. The Jesuits noted the Jews in Kaifeng observed Sabbath from Friday sundown to Saturday sundown. They celebrated all Jewish holidays, circumcised their boys and did not eat pork. They said the same prayers and had all the important Hebrew manuscripts, including Torah scrolls. Although the Jesuits did not look in detail the entire collection of Torah scrolls, they did copy some of the beginnings and endings which were found to be identical to the Hebrew Bible in the west.

Three years following Ricci's meeting with Ai Tian, Ricci wrote to the chief rabbi in Kaifeng, telling him the Messiah they had been waiting for had arrived — Jesus. The chief rabbi replied, saying the Messiah would not come for a long time. The rabbi further offered Ricci his position in Kaifeng, under the condition Ricci would give up pork.

Ricci passed all this information back to Rome, describing these Jews as having been in China "from time immemorial."

Subsequent to the west discovering the community of Jews in Kaifeng, many missionaries visited and tried to convert them. So far, no record of baptism has been found.

12.6

Kaifeng Torah Scrolls & Missionaries

The Jesuits had a theory that the "original" Old Testaments contained passages foretelling the coming of a Christian messiah, in language so explicit that even the Jews had to accept Jesus as the true Messiah. They suspect these relevant sections had been removed by the Jews. They believed if they were proved right, there would be a mass conversion to Christianity.

Figure 41 A well-guarded Torah scroll at the home of a modern Kaifeng Jew. [Nicholas Zane Archives]

The Jesuits believed the Kaifeng Jews might be different. Due to their extensive isolation in China, they lacked a strong connection with the mainstream Jewish world in the west.

They were also not aware of the existence of Christianity, as per Matteo Ricci. They came to China before the birth of Christ, brought with them Torah scrolls from the pre-Christian era, and had no motivation to make any changes. The Kaifeng Torah might, therefore, be the "original", untampered holy manuscript. Thus, the Jesuit missionaries were extremely keen to obtain a copy to verify their theory.

The Jesuits tried on many occasions to either take a look at the Kaifeng Torah or buy the Kaifeng Torah. The Kaifeng Jews time and again refused their request, claiming only the rabbi was allowed to enter the Holy of Hollies and touch the scrolls; and that these holy books were definitely not for sale. The Jesuits offered financial assistance to the community, even to upgrade and expand the synagogue as an exchange. Unfortunately, their requests were met with only rejections, until the middle of the 19th century. (For more, see Qing Dynasty.)

When the Jesuits finally had full access to the holy text, they were disappointed to find out there was no difference between the Kaifeng Torah and the European Torah.

Figure 42 Kaifeng Jews no longer have in their possession the ancient Torah scrolls from their forefathers. Instead, they try to collect whatever they can to re-connect themselves to their place of origin, as displayed in this Kaifeng Jew's home. [Nicholas Zane Archives]

12.7

Theory on When Jews Arrived China

During Matteo Ricci's many interactions with the Kaifeng Jews, he learnt not only did the Kaifeng Jews not celebrate Hanukkah, they were not even aware of its existence. This lead to the theory that Jews might have left holy land and settled in China sometime around the second century BC, prior to the Maccabean Revolt (167–160 BC) and the origin of Hanukkah (For more, see Han Dynasty.)

Figure 43 [אליעד מלין]

12.8

Flood of 1642

The Yellow River flood of 1642 was devastating to the city of Kaifeng and the Kaifeng Jews.

Kaifeng was located on the southern bank of Yellow River. With ground level 10 meters (33 feet) below the river bed, Kaifeng had seen more than its fair share of violent floods.

Figure 44 Yellow River Flood. [Liu Hongda, Xinhua]

The 1642 flood, however, was a man-made disaster.

By the mid-1400s, the Ming Dynasty had perfected a flood-control system that generated great success for over a century.

In 1642, the dykes were deliberately busted by Ming army, hoping the floodwater would break a six-month siege on the city of Kaifeng by peasant rebel leader Li Zicheng. The Siege did end, but the flood also killed roughly half of Kaifeng's

600,000 residents. The ensuing famine and plague lead to even more death.

This was the most destructive event in the history of Kaifeng Jews. It destroyed the synagogue, submerged the Torah and other sacred texts, and scattered the community.

12.9

Other Jewish Communities in China

Before the end of the Ming Dynasty (1644), there were several other Jewish communities in China. It is still unknown how all these communities eventually perished.

HANGZHOU (杭州)

Figure 45 [chinahighlights.com]

Hangzhou became an important city in Chinese history when the Sui Dynasty (隋朝, 581–618) made it the southern terminus of the Jing-Hang Grand Canal (京杭大运河). The Grand Canal connected Hangzhou (杭州) to Beijing (北京), passing through the provinces of Zhejiang (浙江), Jiangsu (江苏), Shandong (山东) and Hebei (河北). It also linked the Yangzi River (长江) to the Yellow River (黄河), completely flourished inland trade and prospered China. It is still the longest and oldest man-made river in the world.

When the Northern Song Dynasty (北宋,960–1127) was defeated by the Jin Dynasty (大金,1115–1234), a large portion of the Kaifeng population moved with the Imperial

Court to Hangzhou, the capital of the Southern Song Dynasty (南宋, 1127–1279). Many Jews followed this move.

An Arab explorer and scholar named Ibn Battuta visited Hangzhou in 1346. He recorded that he entered the city via the "Jews Gate", alarming to him the existence of Jews in the vicinity.

During their meeting in 1605, Ai Tien told Matteo Ricci that there once was a large community of Jews in Hangzhou and that they even had their own synagogue.

NINGBO (宁波)

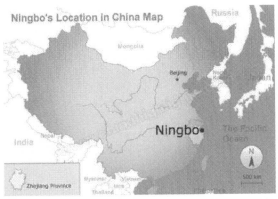

Figure 46 [chinahighlights.com]

When the Ming Dynasty (明朝, 1368–1644) closed off Silk Road by land, Ningbo became an important trading port for the Maritime Silk Road.

The 1489 stone tablet mentioned that the Jewish communities of Ningbo and Kaifeng had a very good relationship with each other and that when the Kaifeng Jews lost their holy texts to the flood, the Ningbo Jews presented their brethren in Kaifeng with two Torah scrolls in 1461. The tablet detailed, "When the synagogue was rebuilt, Shi Bin, Li Rong, and Gao Jian, and Zhang Xuan went to Ningbo and brought back a scroll of the Scriptures. Zhao Ying of Ningbo brought another scroll to Kaifeng and respectfully presented it to our synagogue".

It is believed the Ningbo Jewish community was fairly sizeable for a smaller one would not be able to spare two Torah scrolls. The availability of these scrolls could also mean the Ningbo Jewish community was vibrant and observant.

YANGZHOU (扬州)

Figure 47 [chinahighlights.com]

Yangzhou, also located at the southern terminus of the Grand Canal (大运河), was the headquarter of the salt administration during the Tang Dynasty (唐朝, 618–907). The salt traders became immensely wealthy and Yangzhou flourished as a trading centre.

The 1512 stone tablet mentioned the Jews in Yangzhou donated a Torah Scroll and funded the building of a second gateway to the Kaifeng synagogue. It is also believed that the 1512 inscription was written by a resident of Yangzhou.

NINGXIA (宁夏)

Figure 48 [chinahighlights.com]

Ningxia was where mountains and deserts met the Yellow River, a key caravan stop along the ancient silk road that connected China to Central Asia. This was where China conducted active culture and goods exchanges with the Arab world.

Both the 1489 and 1512 stone tablets mentioned a Jewish community in Ningxia. The 1489 tablet noted that the Jin clan was of high social standing in Ningxia. One member of the clan, Jin Xuan donated an altar, numerous vases and candles to the Kaifeng synagogue in its rebuilt after a flood. His younger brother, Jin Ying, funded the production of the stone tablet. The 1512 tablet stated that a Jin Ren from Ningxia sponsored part of the fund needed for the expansion of the Synagogue.

From this, it is possible to deduce that the Ningxia Jewish community and the Kaifeng Jewish community were close to each other, over an extended period of time.

BEIJING (北京)

Figure 49 [chinahighlights.com]

The Yuan Dynasty (元朝, 1271–1368), being the first foreign dynasty to rule all of China, made Beijing its capital and Beijing became, for the first time, the capital of entire China.

Marco Polo, the famous Italian traveller, lived in China from 1275 to 1292. He worked as a special advisor and envoy for Yuan's founding emperor, Kublai Khan. Marco Polo wrote about China's astonishing size and prosperity and that Chinese people had "all things in great abundance." He recorded there were Jews in Beijing in 1286 and that Emperor Kublai Khan showed much respect for their religion.

13. 清朝 Qing Dynasty (1644–1912)

Figure 50 [Minneapolis Institute of Arts]

The Manchus who founded the Qing Dynasty were fond of Chinese civilisation. They worshipped Buddhism, respected Taoism, and based many of its ruling policies on Confucianism. During its ruling period, there were five large Muslim rebellions which were brutally suppressed by military force. Since most Chinese did not know the difference between Jews and Muslims, the Jews had to hide their Jewish identity in order to avoid oppression.

13.1

Synagogue Rebuilt & Stone Tablet of 1663

After the complete destruction of Kaifeng in 1642, the city was abandoned until 1662 when Qing Emperor Kangxi (康熙帝爱新觉罗玄烨, 1661–1722) rebuilt it. Kaifeng never regained its previous glory, it became a rural backwater of minimum importance.

In 1663 the synagogue was rebuilt under the direction and financial support of a Jew, Zhao Yingcheng (赵映乘; Hebrew name: Moshe ben Abram), with help from his brother, Zhao Yingdou (赵映斗).

The Zhao brothers were fluent in both Hebrew and Chinese. They passed the civil service examinations and were highly ranked mandarins in the Imperial Court. Together, they gathered the scattered Jews and assisted them in relocating back to their previous homes.

The Kaifeng Jewish community erected a stone tablet to commemorate the new synagogue. The tablet described Zhao Yingcheng as "fearing that the members of the religion, owing to the ruin of synagogue might disperse and never come together again, and unable to contemplate the work his ancestors had built up and preserved through the centuries suddenly destroyed in a single day … sent troops to patrol and protect the remnants of the synagogue day and night."

The tablet also told that the Zhao brothers traced down "the actual foundation of the former synagogue" which was covered under heavy Yellow River silt, and therefore set the location on which the new synagogue was built.

The tablet inscription illustrated the shared value system between Judaism and Confucianism — a life of service, emphasis on family, tradition and education. It captured the rebellion of Li Zicheng (李自成), the fall of Ming Dynasty and the founding of Qing Dynasty.

It described the incredible difficulty the community faced during the dynastical transition when the synagogue was destroyed by the rebels and anything of value looted; but optimistically concluded that despite all the chaos, the community stayed together and hang on hard to their religion.

Unfortunately, this stone tablet disappeared in 1912, along with the last of Chinese dynasties.

Thirteen hand-copied Torah scrolls, mostly donated by other Jewish communities in China, were eventually placed inside this new synagogue.

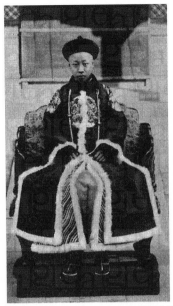

Figure 51 The last Emperor of China, Aisin Gioro Puyi (爱新觉罗溥仪), was forced to abdicate his throne in 1912, the year the 1663 stone tablet disappeared. [Public domain]

13.2

Structure of Synagogue

Emperor Yongzheng (雍正帝爱新觉罗胤禛, 1723–1735) found the concept of having his subjects being loyal to the Pope rather than to him unacceptable. In 1723, he passed a decree to ban Catholicism and deport all missionaries from China.

Just before the ban, in 1722, Father Jean Domenge visited Kaifeng. He recorded extensively Jewish life in Kaifeng and sent everything back to Rome.

Father Domenge made detailed sketches of both the interior and exterior of the synagogue and noted that the Jewish community took extreme care and great pride in the maintenance of their house of worship. He observed that the synagogue was very Chinese in architecture, with courtyards, wood carvings and strong bilateral symmetry.

The synagogue was decorated by many large trees. Typical of local tradition, the main entrance was closed all year round except during Chinese New Year time. People normally entered the synagogue by the two side doors. The Holy of the Holies was a special room that no one except the rabbi could enter, and only during special times of the year. The stone tablets were placed in a visible spot to the right-hand side of the courtyard.

Figure 52 The Kaifeng Synagogue. Original sketch by Father Domenge in 1722. [Nicholas Zane Archives]

The synagogue was called the Temple of Purity and Truth (清真寺) by the locals, the same name they used in referring to the Muslim mosques. The synagogue had a separate hall for ritual slaughter. Special booths were decorated and dedicated to their well-known ancestors, and incense sticks were burned in honour of their patriarchs Abraham, Isaac and Jacob.

It was further recorded that there were 13 copies of the Torah scroll, each enclosed in a silk case. On Sabbath, the Jews had the tradition of placing the Torah on a special "chair of Moses" before reading it. Above the chair hung a plaque that said, "Long live the Emperor (皇上万岁)," a requirement for all places of worship by the Imperial Court.

The Jews were wise — in Hebrew characters which the Chinese could not understand, above plaque, they placed the Shema. The Shema stated, "The Lord is our God, the Lord alone." With this, the Jews knew in their heart that their God was above everything.

13.3

Destiny of Kaifeng Scrolls

Jesuit recordings showed that even in the early 1700s Judaism was still actively practised in Kaifeng — children were able to read and write Hebrew and rabbis were still being trained.

From 1724 to mid-1800s, China turned to isolationism and Kaifeng Jews again lost all contact with the West.

In 1810, the last of Kaifeng's rabbis died. With his death, there was no one in the community who could read Hebrew anymore.

A British government official visited Kaifeng in 1849, he wrote that there were only 1,000 Jews remained. None of them knew any Hebrew and they all looked completely Chinese. The community still tried to maintain a sense of identity and a few Jewish practices remained, such as maintaining their own burial grounds, no mixing of milk with meat, and no consumption of pork, blood and other un-kosher meat. The lack of rabbi, however, meant they no longer knew how to worship or celebrate Jewish holidays properly. In a desperate appeal to stay connected with their roots, they even posted Hebrew books in Kaifeng town centre and offered rewards to anyone who could read it, but no one could.

As China declined politically and economically towards the end of the Qing Dynasty, so did this small community of destitute Jews. Facing extremely poverty, the Kaifeng Jews had no choice but to let go of their most valued possessions. Beginning in 1851, they started selling their Torah scrolls and liturgical books to Christian missionaries, in return for few pieces of silver. The Protestant missionaries purchased and preserved any and all manuscripts they could find.

Of the 13 Torah scrolls that were said to have been held in the Kaifeng Synagogue since 1663, only seven complete sets remained.

They are now preserved in museums and libraries throughout the world, including the British Museum.

Figure 53 A set of Kaifeng Torah, bought by missionaries in 1851 and presented to British Museum in 1852. [Public Domain]

A collection of Jewish Prayer books written in Hebrew and Chinese characters can be found in the library of the Hebrew Union College in Cincinnati, Ohio. The collection includes portions of the Torah and prayer books. The payer books for the Sabbath, estimated to be from the Ming Dynasty (1368–1644), contained the names of the participants. The manuscripts were acquired in the 1920s from a missionary society.

Figure 54 Ming Dynasty Sabbath prayer book with men's names —— from the Zhao clan, in Hebrew and Chinese. Collection from the Hebrew Union College in Cincinnati, Ohio. [huc.edu]

Figure 55 Ming Dynasty Sabbath prayer book with women's names in Hebrew and Chinese. Collection from the Hebrew Union College in Cincinnati, Ohio. [huc.edu]

It is said that a collection of holy text ended up on Hong Kong's antique market, Cat Street in the 1970s and are now housed in Hong Kong's Ohel Leah Synagogue.

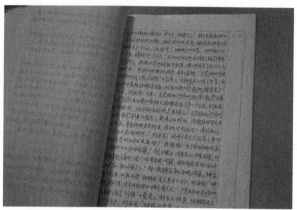

Figure 56 Hand-copied Torah page in Chinese, by the modern Kaifeng Jews. [Nicholas Zane Archives]

Figure 57 A complete set of hand-copied Torah in Chinese, stored in the Kaifeng Jewish History Memorial Center. [Nicholas Zane Archives]

13.4

Final Destruction of the Synagogue

The Yellow River flood of 1854 finally swept away the Kaifeng synagogue. It was never rebuilt. The Kaifeng Jews scattered into China's vast countryside, very few returned this ravaged city.

Figure 58 The Zhao clan came back to their ancestral home after the flood of 1854 receded.
[Kaifeng Jewish History Memorial Center]

In 1914, this poverty-stricken community sold the site of their beloved synagogue to an Anglican Bishop and parted with the land they had worshipped upon for over 700 years.

The only remnant today of the synagogue is a water-well which was closed off in 2014.

Jiao Jing Hutong, or Teaching Torah Lane, a street on which Jews centred themselves during the glory days of the synagogue, lives now only the Zhao clan.

Figure 59 Kaifeng's street sign — North Teaching Torah Lane. [Nicholas Zane Archives]

Figure 60 Though no longer visible, the Kaifeng Synagogue is still in the heart of many Kaifeng Jews, its location easily identifiable. [Nicholas Zane Archives]

The Kaifeng Synagogue now sleeps, buried beneath 10 feet of Yellow River's silt. Above it sits the Kaifeng Chinese Medicine Hospital.

Figure 61 Ten feet beneath this gate lies the main entrance to the buried Kaifeng synagogue.
[Nicholas Zane Archives]

PART III

MODERN CHINA

14. Modern China

In China, the Jews have always found a safe place from the pervasive anti-Semitism found elsewhere in the world. The major faiths of China — Buddhism, Taoism, and Confucianism — are all philosophical schools of thought and practices which do not have conflicts of interests with Judaism, as did Christianity and Islam in the west. Furthermore, the Jews were able to live in harmony with the Chinese because of shared values, such as emphasis placed on education and respect for the elderly — filial piety and 'honour thy father and thy mother'.

Today, they share even more. The Chinese and the Jews both experienced unfathomable suffering during World War II — six million Jews died in the hands of the Nazis, whilst 35 million Chinese perished in the hands of the Japanese.

Modern China is often defined to have begun at the outset of the First Opium War when China was forced to open its door to international trades. Therefore, Jews who immigrated to China after the war can be thought of as Modern Jews in China.

Figure 62 First Opium War — Destroying the Chinese war junks. [Edward Duncan]

The Jews who arrived in China (Kaifeng, in particular) before the First Opium War are physically indistinguishable from their Han neighbours because of generations of intermarriage. However, the Jews who arrived in China after the First Opium War did not intermarry and therefore remained ethnically different from Han Chinese citizens.

This new wave of Jews, upon enlightenment, did indeed reach out to their Jewish brethren in Kaifeng, hoping to help them re-discover their Jewish heritage and reconnect with their Jewish roots.

Figure 63 Shanghai Jewish Chronicle, published in German, ran from 1937 to 1945.
[Shanghai Jewish Refugee Museum]

The category of Jews who entered Modern China can be divided into three waves. The first wave comprised of Sephardic Jews who came from Iraq and India to gain wealth and create business empires; the next wave were Ashkenazi Jews who, seeking to escape the Pale of Settlements and the anti-Semitic atmosphere of the Romanov Dynasty, travelled eastwards and ended up in China; finally, came another wave of Ashkenazi Jews who similarly sought refuge from anti-Semitism — these Jews were fleeing Hitlerism.

15. First Opium War

Opium was first introduced to China in the 17th century, in the form of madak, a blend of opium with tobacco smoked with bamboo pipes. Countless smoking dens popped up along the Southern coastal cities and were viewed as corrupting the Chinese both morally and physically. In 1729, Qing Emperor Yongzheng (雍正帝爱新觉罗胤禛) banned the smoking of madak. British merchants complied.

During this period, China's interest in Western goods was very limited whilst European demand for Chinese silk and tea was insatiable. They loved the texture and beauty of silk and they found drinking tea prevented them from getting sick — instead of drinking water straight out of lakes and rivers, tea called for boiling the water first which assisted in killing bacteria and germs; however, this was not common knowledge at the time and the European contributed the health effect of drinking disinfected water to tea. The large trade deficit drained Europe of its silvers, as this was the only form of currency acceptable to the Chinese.

By 1780, the added pressure from the British East India Company's rapidly deteriorating financial health made Britain re-evaluate and subsequently resume opium trading, despite any Chinese legislation. The British grew opium in its tropical countries, namely India, and sold it to the Chinese. By 1800, the British East India Company dominated this supremely lucrative opium market in China.

Figure 64 An opium den in China. [Public Domain]

In the 1830s, over 20,000 chests, each containing about 75 kilograms of opium, arrived annually in Canton, the only port open to foreign trade. Chinese consumption skyrocketed except this time, instead of madak, they smoked pure opium. The drastic increase in narcotic addicts, plus the rapid outflow of silver, caused grave concern for the Qing Imperial Court.

In 1838, Emperor Daoguang (道光帝爱新觉罗绵宁, 1820–1850) appointed special commissioner Lin Zexu (林则徐) to ban the illegal import of opium. After a letter sent to Queen Victoria of the United Kingdom pleading for a stop to the opium trade was ignored, Lin confiscated and destroyed over 20,000 chests of opium and ordered a blockade of European ships to prevent more opium from coming into Canton.

The British retaliated with military force which resulted in a devastating defeat for the Chinese and the signing of the Treaty of Nanking in 1842. In addition to pay a large indemnity and hand Hong Kong to Britain, four additional ports — Xiamen, Fuzhou, Ningbo and Shanghai — were forced open to foreign trade. The treaty furthermore exempted all foreigners from Chinese law, meaning their degree of freedom was so significant they were essentially above the law.

Figure 65 Commissioner Lin Zexu destroying opium outside of Humen port (虎门销烟).
[chinesegeography.skyrock.com]

16. First Wave of Immigrants — Shanghai

The first wave of Jewish immigrants to modern China was the Sephardic Jews from Iraq and India. Their story is closely related to that of the Sassoon family. David Sassoon, treasurer of Baghdad between 1817 and 1829, moved from Baghdad to Bombay in 1832. He later became the leader of the Baghdadi Jewish community in Bombay. As British citizens, the family enjoyed exemption from Chinese laws and soon became dominant players in the trading of cotton and opium.

After the Treaty of Nanking, David Sassoon sent his sons to the newly opened treaty ports — Xiamen, Fuzhou, Ningbo and Shanghai — which, as new colonial outposts, was subject to lower tax rates, less competition, and less prejudice. David Sassoon's elder son, Abdullah Sassoon, remained in Bombay to supervise the family's existing business. The second son, Elias Sassoon, moved to Shanghai in 1850 in hopes to making it big in the far east.

Figure 66 David Sassoon (seated) and his sons Elias David, Albert (Abdallah) & Sassoon David. [Public Domain]

The family made a huge fortune by selling opium produced in India to China in exchange for tea, silk and other commodities, which were then shipped to England. By the 1870s, the Sassoon family was the leading importer of opium into China. With extreme foresight, they also bought land at unbelievably low prices; when the price rose in the following decades, the Sassoon family reaped large financial gains.

In 1921, the Sassoons constructed the Ohel Rachel (拉结会堂) with a seating capacity of 700 people. Thirty Torah scrolls were placed inside. The compound included a library, a playground and a ritual bath. It replaced the Beth El Synagogue which was built in 1887.

In 1943, the Japanese created the Restricted Sector for Stateless Refugees (无国籍难民限定地区) in the Hongkou district (虹口区). The Jews had to leave behind their beloved synagogue and move to the Shanghai Ghetto (上海难民营). Ohel Rachel was subsequently converted into a stable.

In 1949, with the founding of the People's Republic of China, the Communist Party allowed the Jewish community to continue using the Ohel Rachel until 1952 when the synagogue was took over and stripped most of its interior furnishings. During the Cultural Revolution, the building was use as a warehouse. In 1994, the Shanghai government made it a protected architectural landmark of the city.

Figure 67 Ohel Rachel. [Nicholas Zane Archives]

Today, the Ohel Rachel is used by the Shanghai Association of Higher Education (上海市高等教育学会) and closed to the public. Out of the original six, it is one of the only two synagogues still standing in Shanghai.

Sir Victor Sassoon, grandson of Elias David Sassoon, transferred much of the family's wealth from India to Shanghai in the 1920s and 1930s. At one time, the family owned over 1,800 properties in Shanghai, including some of the most significant landmarks in Shanghai — the Cathay Hotel and the Cathay Theatre.

Figure 68 The Fairmont Peace Hotel. [Nicholas Zane Archives]

In 1929, Sir Victor Sassoon opened the Cathay Hotel — now called the Fairmont Peace Hotel (上海和平饭店), setting an absolute new height and luxury standard for all of Asia. Situated at the intersection of the Bund and Nanjing Road — Shanghai's busiest shopping street, this was the Sassoon's grandest and most iconic masterpiece. It was also Shanghai's first American-style, art deco skyscraper. Just below its copper-green, pyramid-shaped roof, on the 11th floor, was Sir Victor's penthouse.

It was in this hotel that the most decadent tea dances, costume parties and grand balls were held, attracting socialites and celebrities from all over the world. Some speculated that Sir Victor's extravagant parties were partly inspired by his spite for the many Shanghai clubs that denied him entry — because he was a Jew. His sarcastic response to the anti-Semitic world around him was to make them clamour for invitation to his opulent, air-conditioned ballroom which was designed to resembled the inside of a synagogue.

Figure 69 Interior of the Grand Ballroom at the Fairmont Peace Hotel. [Nicholas Zane Archives]

During the occupation of Shanghai in the late 1930s, the Cathy Hotel was taken over and occupied by the Japanese. In 1956, the hotel reopened under the name of Peace Hotel. It was one of the only two hotels in China at the time that was allowed to accommodate foreign envoys. During the Cultural Revolution, the Gang of Four used the hotel as its command centre for the Shanghai Commune. Over its turbulent history, distinguished visitors from Charlie Chaplin, Cornelius Vanderbilt, Chiang Kai-Shek, Ronald Reagan and Bill Clinton have all stayed here.

In 1949, the hotel's legendary Jazz Bar was closed down when China classified Jazz as "yellow music," in the same category as pornography, and was banned completely. At the end of the Culture Revolution, in the late 1970s, no one in China knew how to play Jazz anymore. The Jazz Bar had to call back its original players, all in their 80s and 90s by then, to continue the tradition.

Today, the Jazz Bar is vibrant and busy, playing to the tune of a bygone era. The band members, with an average age of around 80, proudly call themselves the Old Jazz Band.

Figure 70 The Old Jazz Band plays every night at the Fairmont Peace Hotel. [Nicholas Zane Archives]

Victor's Cafe, named after Sir Victor Sassoon, serves a variety of western pastries while occupying the prime people-watching spot on the Nanjing Road. The cafe's signature dish is Sir Victor's favourite chicken curry.

Figure 41 Cafe Victor at the Fairmont Peace Hotel. [Nicholas Zane Archives]

The hotel's main entrance, facing the Huangpu River (黄浦江), is permanently closed because Feng Shui master claimed the front door should not open onto running water to prevent wealthy from flowing out.

Without a doubt, this is the most famous hotel in China.

The Cathay Theatre (国泰电影院) was also a part of Sir Victor Sassoon's real estate portfolio in the 1930s. Located at the intersection of Huaihai Road (淮海路) and Maoming Road (茂名路), this is one of the few Art Deco cinemas that is still operational today.

The theatre opened in 1932 with the screening of American film "A Free Soul", starring Norma Shearer. It was not only the most magnificent and grand cinema at the time, it was also by far the biggest in Shanghai, with 1,080 seats all on one main floor.

Prior to 1949, the theatre frequently featured American and English movies, especially blockbusters from Paramount Pictures Corporation and Metro-Goldwyn-Mayer, making it exceptionally popular among the foreigners as well as the locals. All movies were shown with Chinese subtitles and earphones which gave spoken translation in Chinese. Movie premiers were often screened here and celebrity figures such as Eileen Chang spotted here.

Figure 72 Cathay Theatre (国泰电影院), located at the intersection of Huaihai Road (淮海路) and Maoming Road (茂名路). [Nicholas Zane Archives]

During the Cultural Revolution, the cinema was renamed People's Cinema; much of the original interior decoration stayed intact until this period. In 1979, it resumed its original name of Cathay Theatre. In 2003, the large auditorium was split into three separate screening halls, none of the original interior survived. In the 1990s, the exterior of the theatre was granted municipal preservation status.

Sir Victor Sassoon was also a strong defender of human rights in China and offered tremendous support to the Jews in the Shanghai Ghetto.

The Sassoons were strict Orthodox Jews who worked hard to maintain their Baghdadi Jewish identity. In the early days when Shanghai was still just a tiny fishing village along the Huangpu River (黄浦江) and lacked the infrastructure to facilitate the maintenance of a Jewish lifestyle, the Sassoons hired other Jews from Baghdad and Bombay, provided them with food and accommodation, ensured everyone observed Sabbath and Jewish holidays, and lived according to the Jewish laws. Amongst those who came from Bombay to work for the Sassoons were the Kadoories and the Hardoons who later branched off and started their own extremely successful business empires.

17. Second Wave of Immigrants — Harbin

The second wave of Jewish immigrants to modern China was the Ashkenazi Jews, mostly from Russia. They came to China under considerably worse condition than the first wave of immigrants.

From the reign of Catherine the Great (1762–1798), Jews of Russia were confined to live within the Pale of Settlement (1791–1917), comprised mostly of modern day Belarus, Lithuania, Moldova, and Ukraine.

Life in the Pale of Settlements was exceeding difficult and poverty-stricken. By the turn of the 19th century, five million Jews, or 40% of the world's Jewish population, could be found within the Pale.

Figure 73 A water carrier on the Pale of Settlement. [litwackfamily.com]

An unsubstantiated rumour of Jewish involvement in the assassination of Alexander II (1855–1881) led to significant outbreak of violence against the Jews; these acts of anti-Semitism are known as pogroms. Alexander III (1881–1894) therefore implemented a series of anti-Semitic legislation to deter a similar fate.

Konstantin Pobedonostsev, a close advisor of Alexander III, captured the essence of the regime, "One-third of the Jews will convert, one-third will die, and one-third will emigrate."

From 1881–1920, the never-ending pogroms and the increased official repression against the Jewish population lead to more than two million Russian Jews fleeing the country. Whilst a vast majority fled to the United States and England, some Jews made their way eastwards eventually ending up in the city of Harbin.

Harbin is now the capital city of Heilongjiang Province (黑龙江省), the most north eastern province of Manchuria. It was a small fishing village prior to 1895 and served as the base of Russian military operation in Manchuria during the Russo-Japanese War (1904–1905). For a certain period, Harbin had the largest Russian population outside of the Soviet Union; in fact, at the time of the revolution in 1917, 40,000 of the 100,000 people in Harbin were ethnically Russian. Today, it is often called the "Moscow of the East" by the Chinese although much of the Russian developed city is no longer there.

The Russian Jews came to Harbin in three relatively distinct phases.

17.1

First Phase — China Eastern Railway

When the First Sino-Japanese War (甲午战争) came to a close with Japanese victory in 1895, China as a power was severely undermined and sought to form alliances if it ever needed to challenge Japanese power. China, therefore, looked north and granted Russia permission to construct the Chinese Eastern Railway (东清铁路). The construction of this would provide a shortcut to the tail end of the Trans-Siberian Railway by linking Chita and Vladivostok via Harbin.

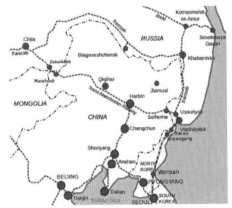

Figure 74 Map of China Eastern Railway (东清铁路). [Voland77]

In order to expedite the completion of the China Eastern Railway, the Russian ruling class encouraged people to move eastwards and take up a role in the railway's construction. They offered the incentive of more rights and privileges, which would not be a lot given the state of the Pale of

Settlements. Nevertheless, 500 Russian Jews who were keen to having a better lifestyle found themselves in Harbin by 1903.

The construction of the railway brought an influx of people to Harbin, as well as a need for all types and goods and services. The Jews grasped onto this opportunity and involved themselves in the development of many industries, including hotels, fur trade, and wood and coal production. The Jews eventually made sure these new businesses reached beyond the borders of China, as they eventually reached the Russian Empire, as well as European countries, Japan, and even the United States.

17.2

Second Phase — Russo-Japanese War

In the early 1900s, Japan offered to recognise Russia's influence in Manchuria in exchange for Russia's recognition of Japan's influence in Korea. Upon Russia's refusal, Japan declared war.

The Russian Jews, although denied of civil rights and confined in the Pale, found themselves at the forefront of conscription; as second tier citizens, they were on the priority list when it came to mustering.

In 1905, Russia lost the 19-month war and lacked the funding to repatriate troops. Demobilized soldiers, including many Jews who were reluctant of returning to the Pale of Settlement, decided to settled down in Harbin.

By 1908, there were about 8000 Russian Jews in Manchuria; in fact, a third of all Russians in Harbin were of Jewish descent. In 1909, the growing population built a synagogue which would come to be the centre of their worship and gatherings. In 2014, this synagogue was refurbished into a concert hall for the performance of classical music.

Figure 75 A postcard of Harbin's Old Synagogue, built in 1909. [Dan Ben-Canaan]

17.3

Third Phase — Russian Revolutions

The Great War (1914–1918), the Russian Revolution (1917) and the subsequent Russian Civil War (1917–1922) brought a sharp influx of Jewish refugees to Harbin. The grandfather of Ehud Olmert, Israel's ex-Prime Minister, fled to Harbin from Russia after World War I, in 1919. When Zionism was outlawed in the Soviet Union, he and his Jewish community in Harbin became the only representative of Russian-speaking Zionists.

Olmert's father, Mordechai, grew up in Harbin where he was a founding member of the local Betar youth movement, an international organisation devoted to the pursuit of a Jewish homeland. Olmert's parents met in Harbin and made Aliyah to Mandatory Palestine in 1933.

By 1920, Harbin was home to approximately 20,000 Russian-Jewish. Between 1920 and 1930, approximately 20 Jewish newspapers were in circulation. This was a time when the Soviet Union was too preoccupied elsewhere to pay much attention to Manchuria and the Jews of Harbin enjoyed the same rights as other foreigners.

Figure 76 Members of Betar Youth Movement, Harbin, 1930. First from the right: Mordechai Olmert. [The Oster Visual Documentation Center, Beit Hatfutsot]

Japanese occupation of Northeast China in 1931 and the creation of puppet state, Manchukuo (满洲国), in 1932 was devastating to the Harbin Jewish community. The Japanese soon became the dominant economic power in the region; the Jews, overshadowed by their new neighbours, struggled financially, leading to emigration to places from Palestine to Shanghai.

18. Third Wave of Immigrants — Shanghai

The final wave of Jewish immigrants, scared by the anti-Semitism of the Nazis, came to China in terror. The Chinese take great pride in this part of history, because during this period Shanghai alone took in more refugees — 23,000 Ashkenazi Jews — than Canada, India, South Africa, New Zealand, and Australia combined.

Figure 77 Shanghai Jewish Refugees Museum (上海犹太人难民纪念馆.) [Nicholas Zane Archives]

Figure 78 Relief Sculpture at the Shanghai Jewish Refugees Museum — six people meant to represent the six million Jews killed during the Holocaust. [Nicholas Zane Archives]

Figure 79 Sculpture Wall at the Shanghai Jewish Refugees Museum — Captures the names of the 13,732 Jewish refugees who lived in Shanghai. [Nicholas Zane Archives]

After Hitler became Chancellor of Germany in January 1933, Jews, previously employed as civil servants and academics, quickly found themselves without a job, whilst Jews running businesses faced nationwide boycotts. Many Jews began to consider leaving Deutschland; indeed, by November of 1933, 26 Jewish families had arrived in Shanghai and had integrated smoothly into their new city.

Figure 80 A Jewish family in Shanghai. [Shanghai Jewish Refugees Museum]

The Nuremberg Laws of 1935 stripped the Jews of their Reich citizenship. Jews were forbidden from marrying Germans and were not allowed to employ German females under the age of 45. Subsequent laws followed which prohibited Jews from attending public schools, going to theatres, and even from being seen in certain districts. Jewish businesses had it worse; troubles which were once boycotts turned into lootings by anti-Semitic Germans.

In March 1938, Germany annexed Austria. Four months later, the United States initiated the Evian Conference, encouraging all 32 invited nations to take in more Jewish refugees; but apart from the Dominican Republic, no country changed its existing stance. This was Nazi gold. Indeed, Hitler and Reich Minister of Propaganda, Joseph Goebbels, seized this as a chance to affirm their verdict that Jews were the scum of the earth that no one wanted in their country.

In November 1938, a Polish Jewish teenager, Herschel Grynszpan, killed a German diplomat, Ernst vom Rath, in Paris. This was used by the Nazis as pretext to initiate Kristallnacht, or the Night of Broken Glass, which saw German paramilitary troops destroy Jewish homes, businesses, and synagogues; in addition to 91 killed in this pogrom, 30,000 Jews were arrested and deported to concentration camps.

This was the existential turning point for the Jews — staying put was no longer an option. Unfortunately, by this time, the United States and many other countries had already closed their doors and denied visas to Jewish refugees.

Figure 81 Germans walk by a Jewish business destroyed on Kristallnacht. [Public Domain]

In 1937, the Battle of Shanghai ended with Japanese victory. Whilst the Japanese took over the Chinese regions of Shanghai, the foreign regions remained under the jurisdiction of Europeans. Shanghai's was divided and left in a mess; no one was in charge, and border control had completely broken down.

As such, although the Jews knew little about Shanghai, other than it was a city far away from home, the option of immigrating to Shanghai to them came as a delight.

Although one did not need a visa to enter Shanghai, it was a prerequisite to leaving Austria. From 1938 to early 1940, Ho

Feng-Shan (何凤山), the Chinese Consul-General in Vienna, issued over 3,000 Chinese visas to Austrian Jews. Indeed, this was done against the will of his superior, the Chinese ambassador to Berlin, who warned him not to do anything that would anger the Nazis.

Figure 82 Ho Feng Shan (何凤山). [Nicholas Zane Archives]

Although there is no official count of Jews who were saved by Ho Feng Shan, it is recorded that he issued his 200th visa in June 1938, and his 1906th by 27th October. Ho Feng Shan was honoured for his services for humanity and, in 2000, recognised by Yad Vashem officially, as he was given the title 'Righteous Among the Nations (חֲסִידֵי אֻמּוֹת הָעוֹלָם)'.

Figure 83 Lloyd Triestino passenger ship (Italian) bringing Jewish refugees from Trieste to Shanghai in the 1930s. [Shanghai Jewish Refugees Museum]

Figure 84 Passenger ticket for the Lloyd Triestino. [Shanghai Jewish Refugees Museum]

Figure 85 Refugees disembarking their ship. [Shanghai Jewish Refugees Museum]

Figure 86 Refugees arriving at the port of Shanghai. [Shanghai Jewish Refugees Museum]

Figure 87 Refugees boarding onto trucks. [Shanghai Jewish Refugees Museum]

Figure 88 Volunteers sending refugees to one of the processing centres. [Shanghai Jewish Refugees Museum]

19. Shanghai Ghetto

Prior to the arrival of German and Austrian Jews, there were already two relatively well established Jewish communities in Shanghai — the Sephardic Baghdadi Jews, numbering roughly 800, and the Ashkenazi Russian Jews, numbering roughly 4,000. Both communities, due to differences in religious practices, were relatively isolated from each other, except when it came to helping out the influx of Jewish refugees.

Between 1938 and 1939, nearly 23,000 destitute central European Jews arrived in Shanghai. The burden to look after them fell completely on the local Jewish communities.

On their arrival, they were often taken directly to the Embankment House which Sir Victor Sassoon, the owner, had already converted into a refugee shelter with a capacity to accommodate 2,500 people. They were able to stay there until they could find permanent lodging elsewhere.

Figure 89 *The Embarkment House was a massive luxurious, curved edifice that extended a quarter of a mile in length. It was the largest building on the coast of China.* [Nicholas Zane Archives]

Figure 90 *The Embarkment House was taken over by the government and turned into government housing. Three floors were added in the 1980s.* [Nicholas Zane Archives]

Dvir Bar-Gal, a journalist and Shanghai Jewish historian said, "to many (Jewish Refugees), the Embarkment Building was their first roof in the new town, until they could find their way out of there to other housing or move to other shelters throughout the Hongkou district." [2010]

Sir Victor Sassoon also endowed a Rehabilitation Fund which provided loans to the refugees to start businesses so that they could become self-sufficient, and help to hire other refugees.

Figure 91 Jewish business in the Ghetto. [Shanghai Jewish Refugees Museum]

Figure 92 Jewish business in the Ghetto. [Shanghai Jewish Refugees Museum]

Figure 93 Jewish business in the Ghetto. [Shanghai Jewish Refugees Museum]

Figure 94 Jewish business in the Ghetto. [Shanghai Jewish Refugees Museum]

Figure 95 Jewish business in the Ghetto. [Shanghai Jewish Refugees Museum]

Figure 96 Jewish business in the Ghetto. [Shanghai Jewish Refugees Museum]

Figure 97 Jewish business in the Ghetto. [Shanghai Jewish Refugees Museum]

Figure 98 Jewish business in the Ghetto. [Shanghai Jewish Refugees Museum]

On October 19th, 1938 the wealthy Baghdadi Jews established the Committee for the Assistance of European Jewish Refugees in Shanghai to provide the much-needed food, housing, education, and medical care to those who could not help themselves. By July 1939, assistance from the American Jewish community arrived in the form of volunteers and financial aid as well.

Refugee life in Shanghai was tough. Harsh weather and inadequate sewage contributed to a high illness and death rate. The Sino-Japanese War and Japanese occupation completely destroyed the economy and wiped out nearly all employment opportunities. The men had even more difficult time adjusting because they mostly came from well-educated and well-respected professional backgrounds; the harsh reality of living on third-party aid was extremely degrading and hard to accept. Interaction with Chinese neighbours, themselves oppressed by the Japanese, was made even more strenuous due to the language barrier and fighting over extremely limited resources.

Figure 99 Jewish life in the Ghetto. [Shanghai Jewish Refugees Museum]

Figure 100 Jewish life in the Ghetto. [Shanghai Jewish Refugees Museum]

Figure 101 Jewish life in the Ghetto. [Shanghai Jewish Refugees Museum]

Figure 102 Jewish life in the Ghetto. [Shanghai Jewish Refugees Museum]

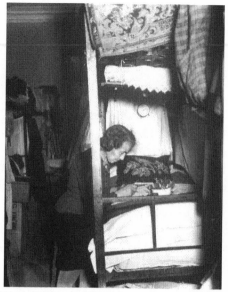

Figure 103 Jewish life in the Ghetto. [Shanghai Jewish Refugees Museum]

Figure 104 Jewish life in the Ghetto. [Shanghai Jewish Refugees Museum]

Figure 105 Jewish life in the Ghetto. [Shanghai Jewish Refugees Museum]

Figure 106 Jewish life in the Ghetto. [Shanghai Jewish Refugees Museum]

179

Figure 107 Jewish life in the Ghetto. [Shanghai Jewish Refugees Museum]

Figure 108 Jewish life in the Ghetto. [Shanghai Jewish Refugees Museum]

Figure 109 Jewish life in the Ghetto. [Shanghai Jewish Refugees Museum]

Figure 110 Jewish life in the Ghetto. [Shanghai Jewish Refugees Museum]

Nicholas Zane

Figure 111 Jewish life in the Ghetto. [Shanghai Jewish Refugees Museum]

Figure 112 Jewish life in the Ghetto. [Shanghai Jewish Refugees Museum]

Figure 113 Jewish life in the Ghetto. [Shanghai Jewish Refugees Museum]

By end of 1939, the Jewish communities took care of the basic needs of almost 16,000 refugees.

On 7th December, 1941 Japan attacked Pearl Harbour and officially entered the Second World War. The Japanese took over the foreign concessions and now took control of the entire Shanghai. They ended all foreign aid, including that of the American Jewish Community.

The Baghdadi Jews were sent to work camps on the outskirts of Shanghai where they were over-worked, underfed and housed in extremely cramped accommodations. The Russian Jews, together with other European residents in Shanghai, not only were sent to work camps but were also required to wear armbands to identify themselves and had their movements being monitored and restricted.

The large mansions owned by the Baghdadis were now occupied by the Japanese troops. Their assets were confiscated and their businesses came to a complete halt. Many Baghdadis resorted to selling their valuables to sustain a living. The Jewish community in Shanghai completely fell apart.

Figure 114 [White Horse Cafe, Shanghai]

By February 1943, the Japanese established the Shanghai Ghetto (上海难民营), officially called "Restricted Sector for Stateless Refugees (无国籍难民限定地区)", and ordered all Jews who arrived after 1937 to move both their residence and business there. The refugees were kept in this area until the end of the Second World War.

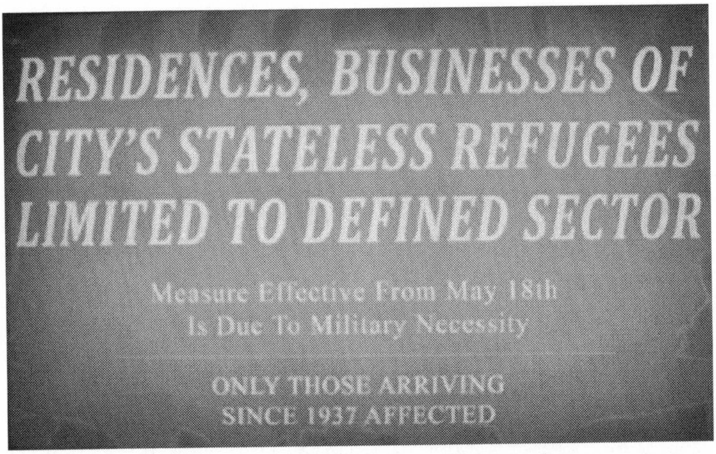

RESIDENCES, BUSINESSES OF CITY'S STATELESS REFUGEES LIMITED TO DEFINED SECTOR

Measure Effective From May 18th Is Due To Military Necessity

ONLY THOSE ARRIVING SINCE 1937 AFFECTED

Figure 115 [Shanghai Jewish Refugees Museum]

Figure 116 Ghetto gate. [Shanghai Jewish Refugees Museum]

Figure 117 Japanese officer in charge of Ghetto pass. [Shanghai Jewish Refugees Museum]

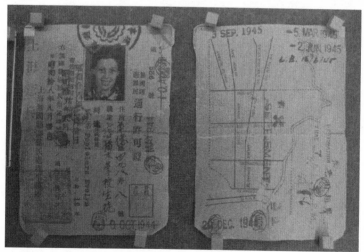

Figure 118 Ghetto pass. [Shanghai Jewish Refugees Museum]

Figure 119 Ghetto identification card. [Shanghai Jewish Refugees Museum]

Figure 120 Ghetto identification card. [Shanghai Jewish Refugees Museum]

With the ensuing Chinese civil war and the establishment of the State of Israel in 1948, almost all Jews who arrived in China following the First Opium War left the country.

Figure 121 [White Horse Cafe, Shanghai]

Figure 122 [White Horse Cafe, Shanghai]

Figure 123 [White Horse Cafe, Shanghai]

20. Kaifeng Jews

In the early 1900s, the Sassoon family, de facto leaders of the Shanghai Jewish community, founded the Shanghai Society for the Rescue of Chinese Jews in order to reach out to the Kaifeng Jews, in hopes of helping them rediscover their Jewish roots and reconnect with their Jewish heritage.

This organisation offered to help the Kaifeng Jews move to Shanghai to become a part of the vibrant, newly established Shanghai Jewish Community. Two Jews, a father and a son, from the Li clan came to Shanghai first. They were later joined by another six Jews. They all expressed a strong desire for financial support in order to rebuild their synagogue.

S. M. Perlmann, author of the book *The History of the Jews in China*, recorded that eight Kaifeng Jews actually came to Shanghai early in 1913 and were shown the proper way to live a Jewish life. They visited many Jewish homes, made many trips to synagogues and watched many Jewish ceremonies. Perlmann observed that the Kaifeng Jews were of "low intellect and lacking education" but able to read the

Bible "thanks to the instructions they had received in Shanghai." He also noted that the Chinese servants in the Shanghai Jewish families were amazed by the way the Jews of Kaifeng were treated: although they were of a low social status they were treated with much respect, as if they were esteemed, high profiled guests.

The organisation tried to teach the Kaifeng Jews to perform ritual circumcision and kosher slaughter. They also planned to provide the resources required to rebuild the synagogue following its destruction in the Qing Dynasty due to flooding. However, Japanese occupation of Shanghai and the influx of refugee from Russia and Central Europe meant the Kaifeng synagogue was no longer a priority for the Shanghai Jewish community. Attention and funds were diverted to more urgent needs.

Figure 124 Corner of a modern Kaifeng Jew's home. [Nicholas Zane Archives]

21. A History of Struggle

From the southern bank of the Yellow River, Kaifeng, to the former fishing village of Harbin, to the most populated city of the present day, Shanghai, there is a Jewish community that remains. Beyond their shared lineage and common ancestry — a tie which bonds them to Abraham, Isiah, and Jacob — these groups share something else in common: a history of struggle.

The arrival of the Jews in each of the three cities is a testimony to this statement. The ancestors of the Jews of Kaifeng, fleeing persecution under the oppressive Antiochus IV, travelled eastwards in making their way to the Silk Road before arriving in the vast Middle Kingdom. Similarly, the Jews of Harbin have an origin that can be traced to a Jewish population facing severe anti-Semitism in the Pale of Settlement — roughly modern day Belarus, Lithuania, Moldova, and Ukraine — under the Russian Empire. These Jews, seeking to distance themselves as much as possible from the heart of the nation took both the construction of the Trans-Siberian Railway and the Russo-Japanese War as opportunities to find jobs in Siberia, eventually settled down in Harbin — often called Moscow of the East. Moreover, when the European Jews sought a place of refuge in a world that was seemingly becoming a living hell because of Hitlerism, these Jews, too, found in China — Shanghai — a haven.

However, the initial struggle that brought the Jews to their three respective cities does not end there. The Jews of Harbin faced further struggle as the Japanese invaded Manchuria in the 1930s, an action which would lead to thousands without a roof above their heads. Indeed, the Jews in Shanghai also had a tough time as they were forced to live in miserable, confined space of Ghetto post-Japanese occupation, with hardly any necessary means for survival.

Whilst the struggles of Jews in Harbin and Shanghai suggest an explicit period of hardship, the problems the Jews of Kaifeng faced were far subtler. The mismatch between the patriarchal nature of Chinese society and the matrilineal structure of Judaism, combined with the intermarriage act which required Jews to marry their Han neighbours contributed to strong cultural dilution during the Ming Dynasty. Moreover, the social hierarchy of China at the time, which highly valued Civil Servants, meant that Jewish families would often deliberately not teach their children about Moses and the Torah, so that more time could be spent on preparation for the Civil Service Examination which required extensive knowledge regarding classical Chinese texts. Indeed, the Chinese surnames the Jews were given during the Ming Dynasty made it harder to track down

Jews through family trees, which would be an emerging problem when events that dispersed the population occurred — frequent floods in Kaifeng. These all contributed to the erosion of Judaism — the religion and the culture — in China.

As such, the history of Jews in China can be categorized by the struggles they faced. Their history is crucial not only because it is fascinating, but the interaction of these two ancient cultures which are often thought of in isolation to one another. This is a perfect example of the big stories that lurk behind the small doors.

Figure 125 Corner of a modern Kaifeng Jew's home. [Nicholas Zane Archives]

REFERENCES

"1898–1914." *Jew of China*, The Jewish Community of China, www.jewsofchina.org/harbin-chronology.

"Antiochus." *Jewish Virtual Library*, American-Israeli Cooperative Enterprise, www.jewishvirtuallibrary.org/antiochus.

"China Virtual Jewish History Tour." *Jewish Virtual Library*, American-Israeli Cooperative Enterprise, www.jewishvirtuallibrary.org/china-virtual-jewish-history-tour.

"Chinas Historic Jews, Synagogue Honoured in Silk Road Exhibit – J." *J Weekly*, The Jewish News of Northern California, 3 Oct. 1997, www.jweekly.com/1997/10/03/china-s-historic-jews-synagogue-honored-in-silk-road-exhibit/.

"Chronology." *Jew of China*, The Jewish Community of China, www.jewsofchina.org/manchuria-chronology.

"Daughter of Late ROC Ambassador Ho Feng-Shan to Receive Posthumous Tribute for Her Father - News and Events." *Ministry of Foreign Affairs, Republic of China (Taiwan)* 中華民國外交部 - 全球資訊網英文網, Ministry of Foreign Affairs, Republic of China (Taiwan) , 7 Sept. 2015, www.mofa.gov.tw/en/News_Content.aspx?n=1EADDCFD4C6EC567&s=31E75C6B67385188.

"Feng-Shan Ho." *Yad Vashem*. www.yadvashem.org/righteous/stories/ho.html.

"Hanukkah." *History*, A&E Television Networks, 27 Oct. 2009, www.history.com/topics/holidays/hanukkah.

"Kaifeng -- Ancient Capital." *China Org*, China Internet Information Center., www.china.org.cn/english/chuangye/41993.htm.

"More than 7,200 Indian Jews to Immigrate to Israel - Times of India." *The Times of India*, Bennett, Coleman & Co. Ltd, 27 Sept. 2011, https://timesofindia.indiatimes.com/india/More-than-7200-Indian-Jews-to-immigrate-to-Israel/articleshow/10140827.cms.

"The Chronology of Shanghai 1832-1932." *Jews of China*, The Jewish Community of China, www.jewsofchina.org/shanghai.

"The History of Jews in China." *Jewish Virtual Library*, American-Israeli Cooperative Enterprise. www.jewishvirtuallibrary.org/the-history-of-jews-in-china.

"The History of the Kaifeng Community." *Jews of China*, The Jewish Community of China, www.jewsofchina.org/chronology-the-history-of-the-kaifeng-community.

"The Maccabees/Hasmoneans: History & Overview." *Jewish Virtual Library*, American-Israeli Cooperative Enterprise, www.jewishvirtuallibrary.org/history-and-overview-of-the-maccabees.

Chen, Stephen. "Why the Yellow River Is so Yellow - and Why It's Prone to Floods." *South China Morning Post*, South China Morning Post Publishers Ltd., 13 May 2017, www.scmp.com/news/china/society/article/2094153/why-chinas-yellow-river-so-yellow-and-why-its-prone-flooding.

Eger, Isaac. "Inside China's Bizarre Obsession With Jews." *Medium*, Medium, 11 Dec. 2018, https://medium.com/s/love-hate/inside-chinas-growing-obsession-with-jews-80bc6ca105bf.

Ehrlich, M. Avrum. *The Jewish-Chinese Nexus: a Meeting of Civilizations*. Routledge, 2008.

Elazar, Daniel J. "Are There Really Jews in China?: An Update." *JCPA*, Jerusalem Center for Public Affairs, www.jcpa.org/dje/articles2/china.htm.

Fontana, Michela. *Matteo Ricci: a Jesuit in the Ming Court*. Rowman & Littlefield Publishers, 2011.

Freund, Michael. "A Millennium of Prosperity on Banks of Yellow
    River." *Jpost*, Jpost Inc. , 26 Sept. 2009,
    www.jpost.com/Jewish-World/A-millennium-of-prosperity-
    on-banks-of-Yellow-River.

Gilad, Elon. "The Obscure Origins and Evolution of the Hanukkah
    Menorah." *Haaretz*, Haaretz Newspaper, 10 Apr. 2018,
    www.haaretz.com/jewish/.premium-the-more-likely-
    explanation-of-the-menorah-1.5346542.

Goldstein, Jonathan, et al. "Detailed History of Harbin." *Sino-Judaic*,
    The Sino-Judaic Institute, www.sino-
    judaic.org/index.php?page=harbin_history.

Guang, Pan. *Youtai Ren Zai Shanghai: The Jews in Shanghai*. Shanghai
    Pictorial Press, 2000.

Guo, Yan. "My Book and Jewish Memorial Exhibition Hall." *Kaifeng
    Jews Memorial Hall*, 29 Apr. 2009.
    http://kaifengjews.blogspot.com.

Heppner, Ernest G. *Shanghai Refuge: a Memoir of the World War II Jewish
    Ghetto*. University of Nebraska Press, 1995.

Hsia, R. Po-chia. *A Jesuit in the Forbidden City: Matteo Ricci 1552-1610*.
    Oxford University Press, 2012.

Ivry, Benjamin. "Why Are the Chinese So Obsessed With the
    Jews?" *Forward*, The Forward Association, 20 July 2016,
    https://forward.com/culture/344669/why-are-the-chinese-
    so-obsessed-with-the-jews/.

Knight, George Angus Fulton. "Maccabees." *Encyclopædia Britannica*,
    Encyclopædia Britannica, Inc., 27 Jan. 2014,
    www.britannica.com/topic/Maccabees#ref72906.

Laytner, Anson, and Paper, Jordan. *The Chinese Jews of Kaifeng: A
    Millennium of Adaptation and Endurance*. Lexington Books, 2017.

Leslie, Donald Daniel. "The Integration of Religious Minorities in
    China: The Case of Chinese Muslims." *Web Archive*, Internet
    Archive Wayback Machine, 1998,

https://web.archive.org/web/20101124011615/http:/islamic
population.com/asia/China/China_integration%20of%20reli
gious%20minority.pdf.

Ma, John. "Re-Examining Hanukkah." *Marginalia LA Review of Books*,
Marginalia Los Angeles Review of Books, 6 May 2015,
https://marginalia.lareviewofbooks.org/re-examining-
hanukkah/3/

Marchant, Leslie. "The Wars of the Poppies." *History Today*, History
Today Ltd., 5 May 2002,
www.historytoday.com/archive/wars-poppies.

Marks, Uri, and Pollak, Lesley. *The Jews of Kaifeng: Chinese Jews on the
Banks of the Yellow River*. Beth Hatefutsoth, the Nahum
Goldmann Museum of the Jewish Diaspora, 1984.

Meyer, Maisie J. "Detailed Shanghai History." *Sino-Judaic*, The Sino-
Judaic Institute, www.sino-
judaic.org/index.php?page=shanghai_history.

Meyer, Maisie J. *From the Rivers of Babylon to the Whangpoo: a Century of
Sephardi Jewish Life in Shanghai*. University Press of America,
2003.

Meyer, Maisie J. *Shanghai's Baghdadi Jews: A Collection of Biographical
Reflections*. Blacksmith Books, 2016.

Minter, Adam. "Return of a Shanghai Jew." *Los Angeles Times*, Los
Angeles Times, 15 Jan. 2006, www.latimes.com/archives/la-
xpm-2006-jan-15-tm-shanghai3-story.html.

Mjl. "The History of Hanukkah." *My Jewish Learning*, My Jewish
Learning, 15 Nov. 2002,
www.myjewishlearning.com/article/hanukkah-history/.

Moore, Charles A. *The Chinese Mind Essentials of Chinese Philosophy and
Culture*. University of Hawaii Press, 1978.

Pan, Guang. "Jews in China: Legends, History and New
Perspectives ." *Kenyon*,

https://www2.kenyon.edu/Depts/Religion/Fac/Adler/Reln2
70/Judaism/PanGuang.htm.

Paper, Jordan. *The Theology of the Chinese Jews: 1000-1850*. Wilfrid
Laurier University Press, 2012.

Platt, Stephen R. *Imperial Twilight: The Opium War and the End of China's
Last Golden Age*. Knopf, 2018.

Pletcher, Kenneth. "Opium Wars." *Encyclopædia Britannica*,
Encyclopædia Britannica, Inc., 13 Feb. 2019,
www.britannica.com/topic/Opium-Wars.

Pohoryles, Yaniv. "The Jews and the Chinese: A Connection between
'the World's Most Ancient People'." *Ynetnews*, Yedioth
Internet, 20 Feb. 2017, www.ynetnews.com/articles/0,7340,L-
4924549,00.html.

Pollak, Michael, et al. "Detailed History of Kaifeng Jews." *Sino-Judaic*,
The Sino-Judaic Institute, 2018, www.sino-
judaic.org/index.php?page=kaifeng_jews_history.

Pollak, Michael. *Mandarins, Jews and Missionaries: the Jewish Experience in
the Chinese Empire*. Weatherhill, 1998.

Poon, Leon. "History of China." *Chaos UMD*, University of Maryland
at College Park, 6 Sept. 1996,
www.chaos.umd.edu/history/toc.html.

Qiang, Ning. "DUNHUANG STUDIES - CHRONOLOGY AND
HISTORY." *Web Archive*, Internet Archive Wayback Machine,
Mar. 2016,
https://web.archive.org/web/20160303192350/http:/www.si
lk-road.com/dunhuang/dhhistory.html

Radovan, Zev, and Josephus Flavius. "Hanukkah: How an Ancient
Revolt Sparked the Festival of Lights." *National Geographic*,
National Geographic Society, 30 Nov. 2018,
www.nationalgeographic.com/culture/2018/11/history-of-
hanukkah/.

Ristaino, Marcia R. *Port of Last Resort: Diaspora Communities of Shanghai*. Stanford University Press, 2004.

Shaw, Annette. "The Evian Conference - Hitler's Green Light for Genocide." *Web Archive*, Internet Archive Wayback Machine, 2001, https://web.archive.org/web/20130827082632/http:/christia nactionforisrael.org/antiholo/evian/evian.html.

Simons, Chaim. *Jewish Religious Observance by the Jews of Kaifeng China*. Sino-Judaic Institute, 2011.

Smith, Mahlon. "Antiochus IV Epiphanes." *Virtual Religion*, American Theological Library Association Selected Religion, http://virtualreligion.net/iho/antiochus_4.html.

Spiro, Ken. "History Crash Course #29: Revolt of the Maccabees." *Aish*, Aish.com, 16 June 2007, www.aish.com/h/c/t/h/48942121.html.

Steinberg, Paul. "Antiochus the Madman." *My Jewish Learning*, My Jewish Learning, www.myjewishlearning.com/article/antiochus-the-madman/.

Van Dyke, Paul, and Susan Schopp. *The Private Side of the Canton Trade, 1700-1840. Beyond the Companies*. Hong Kong University Press, 2018.

Volkmann, Hans. "Antiochus III the Great." *Encyclopædia Britannica*, Encyclopædia Britannica, Inc., 6 Sept. 2016, www.britannica.com/biography/Antiochus-III-the-Great.

Wallbank, et al. "A Short History of the Opium Wars." *Drug Library*, Schaffer Library of Drug Policy, 1992, www.druglibrary.org/schaffer/heroin/opiwar1.htm.

Weil, Shalva. "The Legacy of David Sassoon." *EJewish Philanthropy*, EJEWISH PHILANTHROPY, 30 May 2014, http://ejewishphilanthropy.com/the-legacy-of-david-sassoon/.

Weisz, Tiberiu. *The Kaifeng Stone Inscriptions: the Legacy of the Jewish Community in Ancient China.* IUniverse, Inc, 2006.

Wright, David Curtis. *The History of China.* Greenwood Press, 2011.

Xu, Xin. *Legends of the Chinese Jews of Kaifeng.* Ktav Pub & Distributors Inc, 1995.

Xu, Xin. *The Jews of Kaifeng, China: History, Culture, and Religion.* KTAV Publishing House, 2003.

Zhou, Ruru. "Yellow River Civilization - China's Cradle and Early Capitals." *China Highlights*, China Highlights, 21 June 2017, www.chinahighlights.com/yellowriver/civilization.htm.

ABOUT THE AUTHOR

NICHOLAS Zane

Nicholas is 17 years old. He was born and raised in Hong Kong. At the age of 13 he moved to the United Kingdom to pursue his secondary education.

Through his study of the Holocaust and Russian persecution of the Jews, Nicholas developed a fascination for Jewish history. Upon learning about the story of the Jews in China, which embodied both his interest and his heritage, Nicholas visited all three major Chinese cities with significant Jewish past - Kaifeng, Harbin, and Shanghai. Nicholas founded the student-led organization — *Chinese Jews* — to bring the Jewish diaspora in China's tales of struggle and survival to more people around the world.

Nicholas' interest in Judaism also prompts him to do all he can to combat anti-Semitism, especially given its recent re-emergence and therefore is working closely with many anti-hate organisations.

In order to encourage his peers to do something similar in their own niche, Nicholas also founded an on-line initiative — *Pause for a Cause* — to encourages young people to 'pause' and do something for a 'cause', however significant or trivial.